REEL CULTURE

50 CLASSIC MOVIES YOU SHOULD KNOW ABOUT

(SO YOU CAN IMPRESS YOUR FRIENDS)

This book is dedicated to John Hughes, who brought high school to life,
and life to high school. And to Richard Donner, who showed
the world that behind every geek is a super man.

First published in 2009 by
Zest Books, an imprint of Orange Avenue Publishing
35 Stillman Street, Suite 121, San Francisco, CA 94107
www.zestbooks.net

Created and produced by Zest Books, San Francisco, CA
© 2009 by Orange Avenue Publishing LLC

Typeset in Sabon and Bawdy

Teen Nonfiction/Performing Arts/Film

Library of Congress Control Number: 2009933014
ISBN-13: 978-0-9819733-1-9
ISBN-10: 0-9819733-1-0

CREDITS
EDITORIAL DIRECTOR/BOOK EDITOR: Karen Macklin
CREATIVE DIRECTOR/GRAPHIC DESIGN: Hallie Warshaw
ART DIRECTOR/COVER DESIGN: Tanya Napier
WRITER: Mimi O'Connor
ADDITIONAL RESEARCH: Nikki Roddy
PRODUCTION DESIGNER: Marissa Feind
MANAGING EDITOR: Pam McElroy
TEEN ADVISORY BOARD: Atticus Graven, Lisa Macklin, Andrea Mufarreh, Trevor Nibbi, Sasha Schmitz
Printed in Canada

First printing, 2009
10 9 8 7 6 5 4 3 2 1

Every effort has been made to ensure that the information presented is accurate. Readers are strongly advised to
read product labels, follow manufacturers' instructions, and heed warnings. The publisher disclaims any liability
for injuries, losses, untoward results, or any other damages that may result from the use of the information in this
book.

All photos courtesy of the Everett Collection

REEL CULTURE

50 CLASSIC MOVIES YOU SHOULD KNOW ABOUT

(SO YOU CAN IMPRESS YOUR FRIENDS)

BY
MIMI O'CONNOR

ZEST
BOOKS

Most Iconic Characters p.26

Top Movie Couples p.76

TABLE OF CONTENTS

Legendary
Oscar Moments

p.124

REEL CULTURE

Anyone ever tell you they're gonna make you an offer you can't refuse? Or that they're mad as hell and not going to take this anymore? Wouldn't it be great to know where these expressions came from (hint: movies in this book) and not be in the dark when someone starts gabbing about the twist at the ending of *Planet of the Apes*, the sociological message of *A Clockwork Orange*, or the final shoot-out in *Scarface*?

Classic film references seep into pop culture in ways that many people are not aware of. They pop up all throughout shows like *South Park*, *Seinfeld*, *The Family Guy*, and *The Simpsons*; they appear in newspaper headlines and television commercials; and talk show hosts like

Jon Stewart, Stephen Colbert, and Conan O'Brien bust them out on a regular basis.

The thing is, if you don't know the movie, you're missing out on the joke. At best, you're a little lost and confused; at worst, you might feel kind of like an idiot.

Here are 50 classic American movies from the 20th century that, for whatever reason, just won't go away. This selection begins with something from the late 1930s (when cinema really started seeping into the cultural consciousness) and ends with a flick from the 90s (because later movies are not really "classic"—yet). These are not the best movies of all time or the most popular or the biggest moneymakers—although pretty much every

film in this book would claim a spot on at least one of those lists. But these *are* the movies people riff on and quote, the movies that changed filmmaking and are endlessly name-dropped at parties and throughout the blogosphere.

This book includes everything from famous scenes to quotable lines to little-known trivia about actors, directors, and the making of the films. It also provides plot summaries—including (spoiler alert!) the all-important endings.

Of course, not every great classic movie made the cut. You might say, "What about *Star Wars*"? (Everyone already knows it—if you don't, go rent it. Now.) Or you might wonder why *Bringing Up Baby* is here. (It's one of the best movies of its kind, and every boy-meet-girl flick you've ever seen was influenced by it.) The bottom line is: Every movie mentioned here should be on your must-see list.

Once you come to know these films, you'll be amazed at how many jokes and references you suddenly get. It's like being part of a whole new club. Of course, you might not "want to belong to any club that would have someone like" you "for a member." And after you've read this book, you'll know exactly who said that, in which movie, and when. ★

Mimi O'Con

BRINGING UP BABY

DIRECTOR: HOWARD HAWKS

SCREENWRITERS: HAGAR WILDE AND DUDLEY NICHOLS

WHAT IT'S ABOUT

Dr. David Huxley is a paleontologist one bone away from completing a brontosaurus skeleton and one day away from getting married to his dull and humorless fiancée. He meets Susan Vance, an eccentric heiress who quickly falls in love with him—and someone David quickly decides he needs to avoid, due to the fact that she seems to bring chaos wherever she goes. Desperate to keep him from getting married, she delays and distracts him by insisting he help her deliver a tame leopard named Baby, which was sent as a gift from her brother in South America to her aunt in Connecticut. Exasperated by the ridiculousness of the situation and Susan herself, David agrees, and they set off on a drive from New York to Connecticut. Once in Connecticut, they get caught up in a series of misadventures (many orchestrated by Susan to further delay David's nuptials) that include losing Baby, losing Susan's dog (who makes off with the final dinosaur bone), and ending up in jail. Naturally, they also fall in love.

Who's In It

Cary Grant as
Dr. David Huxley

Katharine Hepburn as
Susan Vance

Charles Ruggles as
Major Horace Applegate

Walter Catlett as
Constable Slocum

May Robson as
Aunt Elizabeth Random

More With Cary Grant

The Awful Truth (1937)
Holiday (1938)
His Girl Friday (1940)
The Philadelphia Story (1940)
Notorious (1946)
To Catch a Thief (1955)
North By Northwest (1962)

★ The dog in the movie is named Skippy; he also played the terrier Asta in the Thin Man movies.

★ The famous ripped dress scene is based on a similar situation that actually happened to Cary Grant when he was at the Roxy Theatre in Los Angeles one night.

WHY ALL THE FUSS?

It's screwball comedy at its finest. A kind of comedy popular in the 1930s and early '40s, screwballs feature absurd situations, slapstick humor, misunderstandings, and witty repartee between romantic rivals and interests. This movie has all of that, and it does it all well.

This is a prime example of a completely American invention: the romantic comedy. Films like *Bringing Up Baby* paved the way for movies such as *Annie Hall* (page 115), *Sleepless in Seattle*, *The 40-Year-Old Virgin*, *The Break-Up*, *Knocked Up*, and many, many more.

Grant and Hepburn's on-screen chemistry was hot and hilarious. The pair's quick, wise-cracking dialogue is considered some of the best in screwball films. Snappy exchanges in this tradition have been seen in the TV series *Moonlighting*, as well as in movies such as *When Harry Met Sally*, *Duplicity*, *Mr. and Mrs. Smith*, *Intolerable Cruelty*, *Leatherheads*, and *Juno*.

Grant's tailored suits and tuxedos and Hepburn's glamorous outfits (including a silver satin dress and fancy night robe) are perfect examples of 1930s Hollywood style.

Bonus Material

★ *Bringing Up Baby* was such a huge box office bomb that director Hawks was fired from the next film he was scheduled to direct for studio RKO. Meanwhile, Katharine Hepburn had a contract with RKO to do several more films, and since she was now considered "box office poison," the executives gave her a terrible assignment for her next film, hoping she would buy out her contract for $220,000 (she did!) so they wouldn't have to buy her out.

Susan and David get friendly with Baby, the leopard.

THE STUFF PEOPLE STILL TALK ABOUT

Grant's exasperated yet cool persona: You can see this dashing tradition still carried out in Hollywood today by stars like George Clooney and Clive Owen.

The dress scene: In a typical slapstick moment, David steps on the back of Susan's dress and rips out the back panel; when she realizes what's happened, she allows him, upon his suggestion, to follow her out of the restaurant to protect her from being exposed.

The bathrobe scene: After Susan has sent David's clothes to the cleaners, he is forced to put on a puffy girly bathrobe he finds in her bathroom. When an older woman rings the bell, the woman asks why he is wearing it. At his wit's end, he says "Because I just went gay all of a sudden!" This is one of the earliest uses of the word *gay* to mean "homosexual," not "happy," in movies.

QUOTABLES

"There is a leopard on your roof, and it's my leopard and I have to get it and to get it I have to sing."

Susan Vance says this to a homeowner who does, in fact, have a leopard on his roof, but doesn't know it and understandably thinks she's crazy.

"Because I just went gay all of a sudden!"

David says this when asked why he is wearing a ladies bathrobe.
(See "bathrobe scene" above.)

THE WIZARD OF OZ

DIRECTOR: VICTOR FLEMING

SCREENWRITERS: NOEL LANGLEY, FLORENCE RYERSON, AND EDGAR ALLAN WOOLF

WHAT IT'S ABOUT

Dorothy Gale is a young girl who lives in the middle of nowhere in Kansas and longs to leave her sleepy life. She gets what she has wished for when a tornado blows through, picks up her house, and drops it in the Technicolor land of Oz. Unfortunately for Dorothy, her falling house kills the Wicked Witch of the East whose sister, the Wicked Witch of the West, is none too pleased. The good Witch of the North, Glinda, gives Dorothy the dead witch's ruby slippers to protect her and directs her to the Emerald City to seek out the Wizard of Oz, who supposedly can help her get back home.

Dorothy sets off down the yellow brick road and along the way picks up some friends who also need help from the Wizard: a scarecrow who wants a brain, a tin man who wants a heart, and a cowardly lion who wants some courage. But the Wicked Witch of the West is still angry and taunts the travelers along their journey with things like fire and sleep-inducing drugs (i.e., potent poppies). In the end, the Wizard can't help Dorothy, but Glinda can, and Dorothy does finally make it back home, wondering if the whole thing was just a dream.

The Wizard of Oz is based on L. Frank Baum's 1900 novel *The Wonderful Wizard of Oz*.

Who's In It

Judy Garland as
Dorothy Gale

Ray Bolger as
the Scarecrow

Bert Lahr as
the Cowardly Lion

Jack Haley as
the Tin Man

Frank Morgan as
the Wizard of Oz

Margaret Hamilton as
the Wicked Witch
of the West

Billie Burke as
Glinda the Good Witch

More With Judy Garland

Broadway Melody (1938)
Meet Me in St. Louis (1944)
Strike Up the Band (1940)
Girl Crazy (1943)

WHY ALL THE FUSS?

As a musical, *The Wizard of Oz* introduced some of the most loved songs in film history, including "Off to See the Wizard," "If I Only Had a Brain," and "Ding-Dong, the Witch Is Dead." Additionally, the movie featured the ballad "Over the Rainbow," which became Judy Garland's signature song. Both "Over the Rainbow" and the entire score won Oscars.

The film skyrocketed Garland from child actor to major movie star overnight.

The art direction was groundbreaking in 1939. The director set the beginning and ends of the movie (the Kansas shots) in black and white, and the middle (Oz) in color, which was still new at the time.

The Munchkinland and Emerald City sets, as well as the costumes (bright silver Tin Man, scary green witch, iconic Dorothy in her checkered dress and ruby slippers), were extraordinarily designed and executed. The costumes, in fact, became iconic and are now Halloween favorites.

Bonus Material

★ Studio execs originally wanted to cut "Over the Rainbow" from the movie (the song is performed during the black-and-white scenes in Kansas at the beginning of the film), thinking the action in Oz should start sooner.

★ Actor Buddy Ebsen was originally cast as the Scarecrow, then was switched to the Tin Man, but he left the production when he discovered he was allergic to the Tin Man's silver makeup.

★ While Judy Garland was not nominated for an Oscar, she did receive an Honorary Award for Outstanding Juvenile Performance for her work. Sadly, after a lifelong struggle with drug abuse, she died at age 47 from an accidental overdose. Her daughter is singer/actress Liza Minnelli.

THE STUFF PEOPLE STILL TALK ABOUT

Dorothy's ruby slippers: They are a symbol of the movie and one of the greatest images from cinema history—they're even on display at the Smithsonian Museum!

The munchkins: The little people Dorothy meets when she lands in Oz, in their town of Munchkinland. The term is now used to refer to small things, among them, doughnut holes from Dunkin' Donuts.

The Wicked Witch of the West: With her green-painted face, pointy nose, and shrill terrifying voice, she was scary then, and she still is.

Dorothy comforts the Cowardly Lion, who's a little short on courage.

QUOTABLES

"Toto, I have a feeling we're not in Kansas anymore."
Dorothy says this as she looks around the fantastical world of Oz for the first time.

"I'll get you my pretty...and your little dog, too."
The Wicked Witch of the West threatens Dorothy, who has just accidentally killed the witch's sister.

"Lions and tigers and bears! Oh, my!"
Dorothy is frightened as she enters the woods on the way to the Emerald City, thinking about what might be lurking in the trees.

"There's no place like home."
Dorothy must repeat this as she clicks the heels of her ruby slippers to get back to Kansas.

1939 GONE WITH THE WIND
DIRECTOR: VICTOR FLEMING
SCREENWRITER: SIDNEY HOWARD

WHAT IT'S ABOUT

It's 1861—in the days leading up to the Civil War—and Scarlett O'Hara is a spoiled, brazen Southern belle who can have any man she wants, but she has her heart set on family friend Ashley Wilkes, who has just decided to marry his cousin, Melanie. In a useless retaliation, Scarlett marries a guy she does not love, who dies while at war. Meanwhile, Rhett Butler, a wise-cracking businessman from Charlotte, starts pursuing Scarlett—but without much luck.

As the war continues, Scarlett's life on the Georgia family plantation they call Tara falls apart quickly. She soon winds up tending to dying soldiers in Atlanta, where she also winds up delivering Melanie's baby. Atlanta gets bombed, and Scarlett, with Rhett's help, takes Melanie and the baby back to Tara, where Scarlett does everything and anything to keep from losing the plantation.

Scarlett and Rhett finally get married, but things go sour and really tank when their daughter is killed in a riding accident. After Melanie dies while giving birth, Scarlett thinks Ashley might finally be hers—but she learns quickly she's been deluding herself all this time. She tries to reconcile with Rhett, but it's too late. Rhett leaves, and Scarlett is now alone, with only one thing to keep her going: Tara.

Who's In It

Clark Gable as
Rhett Butler

Vivien Leigh as
Scarlett O'Hara

Leslie Howard as
Ashley Wilkes

Olivia de Havilland as
Melanie Hamilton

Hattie McDaniel as
Mammy

More with Clark Gable

Red Dust (1932)
Strange Interlude (1932)
*It Happened
One Night* (1934)
The Call of the Wild (1935)

Gone With the Wind **is based on Margaret Mitchell's
1936 novel of the same name.**

WHY ALL THE FUSS?

The movie trounced at the Oscars that year, taking home 10 statues (among them: Best Picture, Best Director, Best Actress, and Best Supporting Actress), and the performances—which definitely seem over-the-top now—were a big reason why.

The chemistry between Clark Gable and Vivien Leigh was hot.

The cinematography—which includes scenes of Atlanta burning and hundreds of dead and dying soldiers—was striking at the time, and still is.

The movie is a saga, nearly *four* hours long, and a powerful piece of historical fiction, setting the romance against the backdrop of a historic, bloody war.

QUOTABLES

"I don't know nothin' 'bout birthin' babies."
Prissy, Scarlett's young servant, says this when it's time for Melanie to give birth.

"You need kissing badly. That's what's wrong with you. You should be kissed, and often, and by someone who knows how."
Rhett says this to Scarlett, at one of their many sexually charged meetings.

"As God is my witness, I'll never be hungry again."
A resilient Scarlett says this after returning from a burning Atlanta to find her plantation in ruin.

"Frankly, my dear, I don't give a damn."
Rhett responds to Scarlett after he has decided to leave her and she asks him, "What will I do?" (In other words: He's over it.)

"Tomorrow is another day."
Scarlett tells herself this at the end of the movie, showing a trace of optimism even after she's lost everything.

THE STUFF PEOPLE STILL TALK ABOUT

Scarlett as an early version of a diva: She has fierce determination and independence, even in the face of tragedy and despair.

The shot of the dead: In a shot created by attaching the camera to a crane to elevate it, the camera pulls back from a group of injured and dying soldiers to dramatically reveal a landscape of hundreds more like them.

The staircase scene: After Rhett and Scarlett have been fighting, Rhett, who is drunk, carries Scarlett up a grand staircase to the bedroom. While it seems like she's fighting him, she wakes up the next morning with a big smile on her face.

Rhett proposes to Scarlett and seals it with a fiery kiss.

★ An old set from *King Kong* was burned for the scenes in which Atlanta is on fire.

★ Every major Hollywood actress tried out for the role of Scarlett O'Hara, including Bette Davis, Claudette Colbert, Jean Harlow, Katharine Hepburn, and Carole Lombard.

★ Oscar-winner Hattie McDaniel was not only the first African-American to win an Academy Award, but also the first to even attend the Academy Awards.

1941

CITIZEN KANE

DIRECTOR: ORSON WELLES

SCREENWRITERS: HERMAN J. MANKIEWICZ AND ORSON WELLES

WHAT IT'S ABOUT

Citizen Kane is about the life of big-time publisher Charles Foster Kane. It begins with a famous scene, in which Kane is about to die. He is in a giant mansion, and a snow globe tumbles from his hand as he utters the word "Rosebud." No one has a clue what that means, but reporter Jerry Thompson goes on a mission to find out.

Through visits with Kane's friends and associates, Jerry learns (illustrated through flashbacks) about Kane's childhood; his unsuccessful run for governor; his failed marriage and pathetic affair with a young, untalented opera singer; his building of a media empire; and his lonely days in old age. In the end, we learn that "Rosebud" was simply a word printed on a sled that Kane played with as a child. Yes, a sled. People have lots of theories about what that means (lost innocence? a lost childhood?), but it surely ties in to the movie's central message: Money cannot buy happiness.

Who's In It

Orson Welles as
Charles Foster Kane

Dorothy Comingore as
Susan Alexander Kane

Agnes Moorehead as
Mary Kane

Ruth Warrick as
Emily Monroe Norton
Kane

More Directed by Orson Welles

*The Magnificent
Ambersons* (1942)
Othello (1952)
Touch of Evil (1958)

Bonus Material

★ Welles' masterpiece was a flop at the box office. It was then nominated for nine Academy Awards (box office success and award nomination did not go hand in hand back then) but was awarded only one, for original screenplay. Every time the film was mentioned at the 1941 Academy Awards ceremony, it was booed.

WHY ALL THE FUSS?

It used innovative (at the time) filmmaking techniques like deep focus (when all images in a frame are in sharp focus), flashbacks, unconventional camera angles, and dark lighting. All of this changed how a movie could look, how a story could be told, and how the psychology and circumstances of a character could be communicated on screen.

Because of the murky, moody lighting in the film, *Citizen Kane* is often referred to as an early example of film noir, a genre that features stark and dramatic black and white photography. Other famed film noir movies: *Sunset Boulevard* (page 28), *Blade Runner* (page 144), *Sin City*, *Blue Velvet*, and *Memento*.

Welles cowrote and directed the film and played the lead role in the movie at age 25.

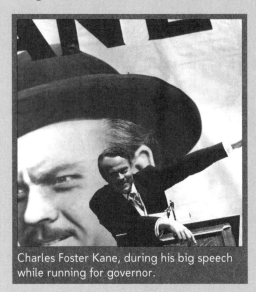

Charles Foster Kane, during his big speech while running for governor.

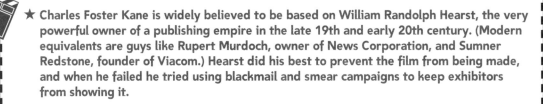

★ Charles Foster Kane is widely believed to be based on William Randolph Hearst, the very powerful owner of a publishing empire in the late 19th and early 20th century. (Modern equivalents are guys like Rupert Murdoch, owner of News Corporation, and Sumner Redstone, founder of Viacom.) Hearst did his best to prevent the film from being made, and when he failed he tried using blackmail and smear campaigns to keep exhibitors from showing it.

THE STUFF PEOPLE STILL TALK ABOUT

Xanadu: Kane's extravagant fortress, in which he died alone. "Xanadu" is now used to refer to an over-the-top estate, typically owned by someone very rich and perhaps somewhat reclusive or eccentric. Some shopping malls and vacation resorts of today have borrowed the name Xanadu.

The sled scene: A young Kane can be viewed out a window playing with a sled in the snow, while his parents, who are inside, prepare to send him off to boarding school. The scene is often cited as a great example of the deep-focus filming technique.

Rosebud: Perhaps the most famous line in movie history (see below). People reference it all the time, and it's been spoofed and invoked on shows such as *The Simpsons*, *The Critic*, *Pinky and the Brain*, and *Mystery Science Theater 3000*.

QUOTABLES

"Rosebud."

This is mysteriously spoken by Kane on his deathbed. The line serves as the jumping off point for the entire movie, as a reporter attempts to figure out what it might mean.

"You provide the prose poems. I'll provide the war."

Kane says this to his newspaper manager, Mr. Bernstein, when he hears from a reporter that there is no war in Cuba. He's basically telling Bernstein to make up stories ("prose poems") to keep newspaper sales up (even though there's no war). This line is seen as a reference to an alleged quote by publishing giant William Randolph Hearst, who was faced with a similar situation while covering the Spanish American War.

1942 CASABLANCA

DIRECTOR: MICHAEL CURTIZ

SCREENWRITERS: JULIUS EPSTEIN, PHILIP EPSTEIN, HOWARD KOCH, AND CASEY ROBINSON (UNCREDITED)

WHAT IT'S ABOUT

World War II is under way and the Moroccan capital of Casablanca has become a gathering place for displaced foreigners, hustlers, and people trying to flee Hitler's regime. (People had hoped they could get visas to Portugal in Casablanca and then travel to the US.) The hotspot of Casablanca is a bar-cafe named Rick's, owned by Rick Blaine, a cynical American.

Rick typically minds his own business, but one day he becomes the unexpected possessor of two valuable visas that will lead to safe passage out of Casablanca. Soon after, Victor Laszlo, a Czech concentration camp escapee and important Nazi resistance leader, and his beautiful wife, Ilsa, come to Casablanca in desperate need of travel papers to get to America. But Rick is unsympathetic: He and Ilsa were madly in love, before the war, in Paris, and she had left him with no explanation. He never really got over it. Now he has the papers—and the power—to decide who leaves Casablanca and who stays. Over the course of the movie, however, he realizes that there is much more at stake than "the problems of three little people." He realizes that Laszlo needs Ilsa by his side in order to keep fighting the good fight, and helps them both escape to America—without him.

Casablanca was based on the 1940 stage play *Everybody Comes to Rick's* by Murray Burnett and Jean Alison. Burnett was a 27-year-old English teacher who had gone to help Jewish relatives in 1938 German-occupied Vienna and then come back to the US to write this play.

Who's In It

Humphrey Bogart as Rick Blaine

Ingrid Bergman as Ilsa Lund

Paul Henried as Victor Laszlo

Claude Rains as Captain Renault

Peter Lorre as Ugarte

More With Humphrey Bogart

High Sierra (1941)
The Maltese Falcon (1941)
The Big Sleep (1946)
The Caine Mutiny (1954)
The African Queen (1951)

More with Ingrid Bergman

For Whom the Bell Tolls (1943)
Gaslight (1944)
Notorious (1946)
Joan of Arc (1948)

WHY ALL THE FUSS?

Humphrey Bogart's Rick is the iconic vulnerable tough guy—the kind of character he became most famous for playing—and Ingrid Bergman is stunningly beautiful throughout the film.

Casablanca is funny, well-written, and also a thriller—you're never quite sure what's going to happen or who's on whose side.

Casablanca was a huge hit when it came out, and it took home several Oscars—for Best Picture, Best Director, and Best Screenplay. (Bogart and Rains were also nominated for awards, as was the music, editing, and photography.)

Rick tells Ilsa, "We'll always have Paris."

★ Although many people think Rick says "Play it again, Sam" in the movie, he really just says, "Play it, Sam."

★ The actors originally slated to star in the lead roles were Ronald Reagan (our former president!) and Hedy Lamarr.

★ Humphrey Bogart was short. He had to wear platform shoes to play next to the very tall Ingrid Bergman.

★ The script was changed frequently throughout production; for most of the filming, Bergman herself did not know if her character would stay with Rick or leave with her husband at the end of the movie.

★ Screenwriters Julius Epstein, Philip Epstein, and Howard Koch were the ones who received an Academy Award for the screenplay. Murray Burnett and Jean Alison always felt this was unfair considering that the movie was based on their play *Everybody Comes to Rick's* (see page 20).

THE STUFF PEOPLE STILL TALK ABOUT

Bogart's belted trench coat and fedora: It's a classic look of an early 1940s tough guy, made even cooler by the fog that fills (somewhat inexplicably, because it's in the desert climate of Morocco) the famous last scene.

The "La Marseillaise" scene: Nazis at Rick's club begin to sing a patriotic German song, and the entire restaurant drowns them out by singing "La Marseillaise," the French national anthem (Morocco is a French territory). It is a patriotic and inspiring moment that unites a random bunch of transients in the face of fascism.

"As Time Goes By": The song that Rick and Ilsa called their own when they were in love.

QUOTABLES

"Play it, Sam."
Rick says this to Sam, the bar's piano player, after seeing Ilsa. He's referring to "As Time Goes By,"
the song he and Ilsa loved when they were together.

*"Of all the gin joints, in all the towns, in all the world,
she walks into mine."*
Rick tells Sam he can't believe Ilsa has popped up in his bar.

"Here's looking at you, kid."
Rick says this to Ilsa at the end; he said the same thing to her back when they were together and happy.

"We'll always have Paris."
Rick is referring to when he and Ilsa were together and in love in France before the war.
He says this before they part forever.

"Louis, I think this is the beginning of a beautiful friendship."
Rick opens up to Captain Renault, who helps Rick at the end of the movie.

1946 IT'S A WONDERFUL LIFE

DIRECTOR: FRANK CAPRA

SCREENWRITERS: FRANK CAPRA, FRANCES GOODRICH, ALBERT HACKETT, AND JO SWERLING

WHAT IT'S ABOUT

This feel-good holiday classic (that has some dark moments as well) tells the story of George Bailey, a man who once had big dreams of leaving his small town of Bedford Falls but never quite made it out. He was just too responsible and constantly making sacrifices for the good of the community and his family. Married to his high school sweetheart, Mary, George is chained to his job running the local bank (which is the family business), and when the bank falls on hard times, George feels all of his sacrifices were for naught and falls into deep despair.

As he is contemplating suicide, George is visited by Clarence, an angel in need of wings, who shows George what the world would be like if he had never been born. George sees a sad, alternate universe in which his brother Harry has drowned, the town has become rundown and is at the mercy of a nasty banker named Henry Potter (it's even been renamed "Pottersville"), and Mary has become a lonely spinster librarian. Finally, George sees the value of his life and becomes grateful for what he has.

It's a Wonderful Life **is based on Philip Van Doren Stern's 1943 short story,** *The Greatest Gift.*

Who's In It

James (Jimmy) Stewart as George Bailey

Donna Reed as Mary Bailey

Lionel Barrymore as Henry F. Potter

Thomas Mitchell as Uncle Billy Bailey

Henry Travers as Clarence

More With Jimmy Stewart

Mr. Smith Goes to Washington (1939)
The Philadelphia Story (1940)
Rear Window (1954, page 23)
Vertigo (1958)

WHY ALL THE FUSS?

📽 It's a fable about the value of family and friends over riches and fame, and it's been known to bring even the most hard-core cynics to tears. Of course, some people find the movie super sappy and annoying, but it still has its place in history.

📽 Its copyright expired in the mid-'70s, enabling television stations to play the movie for little or no cost. The result: *It's a Wonderful Life* was on nonstop during the holiday season (often scheduled as counter-programming to other more commercial shows), which helped cement the movie as a seasonal tradition.

George and Mary in the famous phone scene.

QUOTABLES

"A toast to my big brother, George, the richest man in town."

George's brother, who just returned from the war, proposes this toast in the final scene, after the entire town has raised $8,000 to keep George from going to jail on Christmas Eve. (George was going to jail because of a big financial mistake made by his uncle.)

"Look, Daddy. Teacher says, every time a bell rings an angel gets his wings."

At the end of the movie, George's daughter reacts when a bell on the Christmas tree rings. The tinkling bell symbolizes that Clarence, George's angel companion, finally got his wings.

24

THE STUFF PEOPLE STILL TALK ABOUT

The phone scene: George is on the phone and Mary is listening in on the same receiver. Their faces are very close for a very long time, and they clearly want to kiss each other. (They eventually do.) This was considered hot and steamy for the time and is still thought of as a very romantic scene.

The high school dance scene: George and Mary are at a high school dance, and the floor opens up and dumps all the dancers into a swimming pool below.

Zuzu's petals: During the movie, George is shown what the world would be like without him. At one point in this alternate reality, he checks his pocket for the petals of a flower his daughter Zuzu gave him—they are gone. When George begs to return to his real life—the one he almost chose to end—he checks his pocket for Zuzu's petals and finds them. Today, the phrase "Zuzu's petals" still signifies an appreciation for life and its simple pleasures. The phrase has been used as the name of rock bands, stationery stores, and florist shops.

The snow scene: After he views the grim alternate universe in which he was never born, George returns to his real life and ecstatically runs through the snow-filled town, brimming with joy and loving everything about it that he had come to resent and hate.

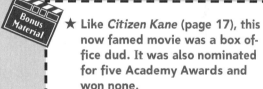

★ Like *Citizen Kane* (page 17), this now famed movie was a box office dud. It was also nominated for five Academy Awards and won none.

★ The script included uncredited contributions from celebrated writers Dorothy Parker, Dalton Trumbo, and Clifford Odets.

MOST ICONIC CHARACTERS

Even if you haven't seen the film, you probably know the character.

★ **Jim Stark,** *Rebel Without a Cause*
This is the James Dean character—a tortured, brooding teenager famously pictured in a red jacket smoking a cigarette. (More on page 34.)

★ **Dr. Hannibal Lecter,** *The Silence of the Lambs*
Anthony Hopkins plays a brilliant and insane serial killer. (More on page 163.)

★ **Norma Desmond,** *Sunset Boulevard*
Gloria Swanson created this delusional and pathetic aging Hollywood diva. (More on page 28.)

★ **Rocky Balboa,** *Rocky*
Sylvester Stallone fought his way into movie history with his portrayal of a working-class under-dog with a huge heart. (More on page 112.)

★ **Harry Callahan, aka Dirty Harry, the Dirty Harry movies**
It's the 1970s and Clint Eastwood is a badass cop who says things like, "Go ahead, make my day."

★ **Joan Crawford,** *Mommie Dearest*
Faye Dunaway portrayed a troubled and abusive real-life movie queen who famously screamed at her daughter, "No wire hangers ever!"

★ **Groucho Marx, the Marx Brothers movies**
Marx's characters never had his name, but they all sported bushy eyebrows, glasses, and a painted-on mustache, and they smoked cigars while spouting wisecracks.

★ **Frankenstein's Monster,** *Frankenstein*
The green guy with the bolts in his neck played by Boris Karloff is technically "The Monster," but everybody knows him as Frankenstein. (Dr. Frankenstein is actually the man who made him.)

★ **James Bond, the James Bond movies**
The slickest, smoothest British spy, who has a way with the ladies and a taste for martinis shaken, not stirred.

★ **Terminator, the Terminator movies**
Arnold Schwarzenegger played this murderous, human-looking machine that could not be de-stroyed. A famous, oft-quoted line: "I'll be back."

★ Rick Blaine, *Casablanca*
Whether wearing a trench coat and a fedora or a white suit jacket and bow tie, Humphrey Bogart's Rick is the quintessential sensitive tough guy. (More on page 20.)

★ Holly Golightly, *Breakfast at Tiffany's*
With her upswept frosted hair, little black dress, and rhinestones, Audrey Hepburn's Holly is the picture of New York party girl glamour and elegance. (More on page 49.)

★ Stanley Kowalski, *A Streetcar Named Desire*
In Tennessee Williams' famous movie, Marlon Brando created the role of Stanley: a steamy thug in a T-shirt who tortures his sister-in-law and, when pining for his wife one night, screams "Stella!" loud enough for the whole neighborhood to hear.

★ The Wicked Witch of the West, *The Wizard of Oz*
Margaret Hamilton is mean, green, and really scary. (More on page 11.)

★ Scarlett O'Hara, *Gone With the Wind*
Vivien Leigh brought to life this fierce, independent Southern diva. (More on page 14.)

★ Darth Vader, the Star Wars movies
James Earl Jones' deep voice combined with an all-black costume that included a weird helmet, plus the sound of heavy, mechanically assisted breathing made Darth an ominous character.

★ Indiana Jones, the Indiana Jones movies
Harrison Ford created this ruggedly handsome, adventure-seeking, fedora-wearing, bullwhip-carrying, wise-cracking archeologist. (More on page 138.)

★ Jason Voorhees, *Friday the 13th*
Once a little kid who drowned at camp, Jason returns wearing a hockey mask and is armed with a machete to get some bloody revenge on some unlucky counselors. (Turns out, his grief-stricken mother is the real killer.)

★ The Tramp, multiple Charlie Chaplin movies
Appearing in silent films such as *City Lights* and *The Gold Rush* and played by Chaplin himself, The Tramp is instantly recognizable thanks to his bowler hat, cane, and small black mustache.

1950

SUNSET BOULEVARD
DIRECTOR: BILLY WILDER

SCREENWRITERS: CHARLES BRACKETT, BILLY WILDER, AND D. M. MARSHMAN JR.

WHAT IT'S ABOUT

Norma Desmond used to be a star of silent movies. Now, she's just old and delusional. She lives with her butler, Max (who was also her first husband!), in a decaying mansion on LA's Sunset Boulevard. In an attempt to have a good movie part written for her, she hires broke screenwriter Joe Gillis to perfect a script she's been working on for ages (featuring her in the starring role). It's not long before he's moved into the house and Norma's become his sugar mama.

When Joe starts getting friendly with another, younger woman, he realizes he's sacrificed his integrity and tries to leave Norma. She threatens to kill herself and notes how much she'll be missed by her adoring fans. Joe finally tells the aging star she's a has-been, and this pushes Norma over the edge into a demented, jealous rage. Determined to keep him from leaving, Norma goes just a bit too far: She kills him. Afterward, in her deranged state, she believes the crowd of people streaming into her house with cameras are there to finally make her great movie. (In reality, it's the press and a lot of cops.) She descends a staircase in costume believing she's about to make her comeback, but she's really about to go to jail.

Who's In It

Gloria Swanson as
Norma Desmond

William Holden as
Joe Gillis

Erich von Stroheim as
Max von Mayerling

Nancy Olson as
Betty Schaefer

Fred Clark as
Mr. Sheldrake

More Directed by Billy Wilder

Double Indemnity (1944)
The Lost Weekend (1945)
Ace in the Hole (1951)
Some Like It Hot (1959, page 43)
The Apartment (1960)

WHY ALL THE FUSS?

- Swanson's portrayal of the deranged Norma went down in history. She defined the archetype of a desperate, aging diva.

- It was the first film to scathingly critique the fickle, superficial world of Hollywood.

- It was nominated for 11 Oscars (including Best Picture, Best Director, and all of the actor categories) and won three.

- It has had major lasting influence: It influenced *Mommie Dearest* and *Whatever Happened to Baby Jane?*, as well as the Broadway hit production of the movie, and the repeated quoting (and satirizing) of its famous lines.

- The celebrity scandal-obsessed culture the movie depicts what was, at the time, an exaggeration. But it no longer is: The movie predicted the paparazzi-like celebrity-hounding culture of today.

QUOTABLES

Joe: "You used to be big."
Norma: "I am big. It's the pictures that got small."
Norma and Joe have this exchange when he first meets and recognizes her from her heyday.

"Mr. DeMille, I'm ready for my close-up."
A completely insane Norma thinks she is filming her next big movie
(Cecil B. DeMille was a major director at the time). In reality, Norma is surrounded by news cameras because she just killed someone.

THE STUFF PEOPLE STILL TALK ABOUT

The underwater camera shot: A scene with a body floating in a pool was shot from an underwater perspective, which was innovative for the time.

The beauty treatment scenes: Norma undergoes numerous ridiculous beauty treatments in an attempt to preserve her youth, and it all makes her look more desperate and ridiculous. (Not unlike many of the aging movie stars of today who've obviously had way too much plastic surgery.)

Erich von Stroheim's acting: He won acclaim for his performance as the devoted butler and former love of Norma.

Joe at work on Norma's movie.

Bonus Material

★ In real life, Von Stroheim was a silent film director and coincidentally had directed Swanson in the movie *Queen Kelly*, which was never released. At one point in *Sunset*, Norma shows one of her previous films to Joe, and it's *Queen Kelly*.

★ Norma's bridge partners in the film, former silent film stars that Joe refers to as "the waxworks," are played by actual stars from that era: Buster Keaton, Anna Q. Nilsson, and H. B. Warner.

★ Aware that studio executives and the Hollywood community might not be thrilled about his movie because it criticized them, Wilder created a fake working title for the film, *A Can of Beans*.

REAR WINDOW

DIRECTOR: ALFRED HITCHCOCK

SCREENWRITER: JOHN MICHAEL HAYES

WHAT IT'S ABOUT

L. B. Jeffries (known as Jeff) is a successful photojournalist who is confined to a wheelchair in his apartment one summer after breaking his leg on a job. Jeff's apartment window faces a group of New York City apartment buildings and, to stay cool, his neighbors keep their windows open. Bored to tears, Jeff becomes obsessed with his neighbors' activities and uses one of his trusty telephoto lenses to get an even better look. Meanwhile, Jeff's girlfriend, Lisa, who is a beautiful fashion model and designer, is trying to persuade him to get married.

Jeff becomes particularly interested in one of his neighbors, Lars Thorwald, whom he suspects may have killed his wife. Jeff's cop friend, Tom, thinks there's a reasonable explanation for all of the "clues" Jeff and Lisa are piecing together, but the couple investigates further, putting themselves in danger. Their sleuthing efforts escalate to the point where Lisa is caught by Lars snooping in his apartment, and when Lars sees Jeff across the courtyard, he heads to Jeff's apartment to confront him. The two men struggle, and Jeff ends up falling out of a window. (Luckily, the police have arrived to arrest Lars and break Jeff's fall, but unfortunately Jeff breaks his other leg.) Amazingly, Jeff and Lisa's seemingly far-fetched suspicions are correct: Lars did, in fact, kill his wife. As a result of the couple's bizarre and scary adventure, their relationship grows stronger as Jeff realizes how much he cares about Lisa and she proves herself to be tougher than she seems.

Who's In It

James (Jimmy) Stewart as L. B. Jeffries

Grace Kelly as Lisa Carol Fremont

Raymond Burr as Lars Thorwald

Thelma Ritter as Stella

Wendell Corey as Det. Lt. Thomas Doyle

More Directed by Alfred Hitchcock

Lifeboat (1944)
Notorious (1946)
Rope (1948)
Vertigo (1958)
North by Northwest (1959)

More With Grace Kelly

Dial M for Murder (1954)
The Country Girl (1954)
To Catch a Thief (1955)

WHY ALL THE FUSS?

Directed by master of suspense Alfred Hitchcock, *Rear Window* is thought to be one of his most suspenseful films. In large part, this is because the hero is wheelchair bound and unable to move.

Rear Window was one of the first movies to explore the theme of voyeurism—the act of achieving pleasure by looking at other people. Later films dealing with the idea are Hitchcock's own *Psycho* (page 46), Francis Ford Coppola's *The Conversation*, Brian DePalma's *Body Double*, and Steven Soderbergh's *Sex, Lies, and Videotape*. The film also cleverly reflects on the concept of a movie audience as a voyeur: We watch Jeffries watching other people.

The movie features Grace Kelly in one of her most memorable roles, in part because she looks stunningly beautiful throughout.

Rear Window remarkably captures all of the elements of a quintessential Hitchcock film—perfectly framed shots, inventive camera moves, and innovative editing.

Bonus Material

★ Instead of shooting in an actual apartment, Hitchcock requested that an apartment complex set be built specially for the film.

★ Hitchcock created a cameo for himself in every one of his movies. In *Rear Window*, he appears in the apartment of the piano player across the way. Read about *Psycho* on page 46 to find out where he appeared in that film.

★ All of the audio in the movie is diagetic, meaning that the film does not include any sound that is not to be heard by the characters.

★ Christopher Reeve—the star of *Superman* (page 121) who was later paralyzed from the neck down in a horseback riding accident—played the Jeffries role from a wheelchair in a 1993 TV remake of the film.

★ The 2007 film *Disturbia* starring Shia LaBeouf is a modern-day take on *Rear Window*.

THE STUFF PEOPLE STILL TALK ABOUT

Kelly's glamorous and elegant attire: She wears ladylike suits and fancy dresses with full skirts, as well as pearls and full-length gloves. She also totes around a famously smart-looking overnight bag by designer Mark Cross.

Lisa and Jeff spy on the neighbors.

The view: Hitchcock masterfully constructed and presented what many city dwellers see out their windows all the time—other people living their lives. Each apartment window provided a look into a wide range of stories, or the stories people project on to strangers from afar: the lonely woman, the frustrated composer, the possibly murderous husband.

The kiss: A sleeping Jeff is awakened by a beautiful Lisa with a very romantic kiss. He then asks jokingly, "Who are you?"

QUOTABLES

"A woman never goes anywhere but the hospital without packing makeup, clothes, and jewelry."

Lisa explains to Jeff why it would be strange for the neighbor's wife to have left behind her jewelry (which they can see) if she was away on a trip.

REBEL WITHOUT A CAUSE

DIRECTOR: NICHOLAS RAY

SCREENWRITER: STEWART STERN

WHAT IT'S ABOUT

It's the early 1950s, and Jim Stark is the new kid at his Los Angeles high school. He feels misunderstood by his parents: His mother is overbearing, and his dad is a total pushover who doesn't give his son any guidance on how to be a man. Almost immediately, a school gang, led by Buzz Gunderson, starts picking on him. The only friend Jim has is an insecure, unstable guy named Plato, who worships him. Jim, however, starts to fall for Buzz's girlfriend, Judy.

Buzz's gang taunts Jim relentlessly, and Buzz starts a knife fight with him one day on a school trip to the local observatory. Things escalate to the point where Jim accepts a challenge of a "chickie run"—a contest of driving cars toward a steep cliff. Jim lives through the contest, but Buzz dies, and when Jim tells his parents about the accident, they just fight among themselves. On the run from the gang, Jim heads to a deserted mansion to hide with Judy in tow. Plato shows up, too, and when the gang members arrive, Plato pulls out a gun and starts firing, hitting one of the thugs. The cops chase the troubled Plato, who runs back to the local observatory. Jim and Judy try to save him, but Plato is shot down by the cops. Jim is devastated, but his father steps up, promising to be someone his son can depend on and look up to.

Who's In It

James Dean as Jim Stark

Natalie Wood as Judy

Sal Mineo as John "Plato" Crawford

Jim Backus as Frank Stark

Ann Doran as Mrs. Stark

Corey Allen as Buzz Gunderson

More With James Dean

East of Eden (1955)
Giant (1956)

WHY ALL THE FUSS?

The movie is one of the most famous portrayals of teenage angst and what was referred to at the time as "juvenile delinquency." Jim, Judy, and Plato all come from homes with distant or absent parents and feel misunderstood by everyone around them. The film struck a chord with the 1950s youth audience when it was released.

Dean's portrayal of the brooding, tortured, and sensitive Jim was praised for its raw emotion, and he became an icon for it.

James Dean is considered to be a total stud and the epitome of cool in this movie.

The film helped to inspire some of the hallmarks of the greaser male teenager: leather jackets, slicked back hair, and fast cars. Others who would later sport this look include Danny Zuko (John Travolta) in *Grease*, the Fonz (Henry Winkler) in the 1970s show *Happy Days*, and Daniel Desario (James Franco) in *Freaks and Geeks*. Franco played Dean in a 2001 made-for-television movie called *James Dean*.

Sal Mineo and Natalie Wood received Supporting Actor Oscar nominations, and the screenplay was nominated for an Academy Award as well.

QUOTABLES

"You're tearing me apart! You say one thing, he says another, and everybody changes back again!"

After Jim has been arrested for public drunkenness, his parents arrive at the police station and proceed to bicker. This is Jim's reaction.

THE STUFF PEOPLE STILL TALK ABOUT

The "chickie run" scene: The face-off between Buzz and Jim ends with unexpected tragedy.

Jim in his red jacket: One of the most famous images of Dean is as Jim Stark, with a white T-shirt and red jacket with the lapels turned up.

The observatory in the film: It's a real place (Griffith Observatory) and is located in Los Angeles.

The concept of being chicken: Jim is repeatedly taunted by people calling him a chicken (a coward), and it's the thing that most gets under his skin.

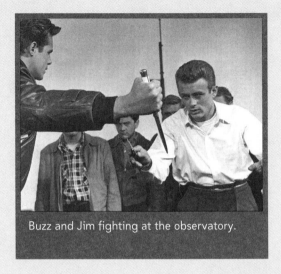
Buzz and Jim fighting at the observatory.

★ Director Ray thought Wood might not be tough enough to play the role of Judy. He reconsidered when she was involved in a car accident while hanging with some Hollywood ruffians, one of which was Dennis Hopper.

★ Dean and Allen used real switchblades for their knife fight scene, but they wore metal armor under their clothes to protect themselves.

★ Paula Abdul's video for her 1992 song "Rush, Rush" is a direct reference to *Rebel* (including many of the same shots); and it casts Abdul in the Wood role and Keanu Reeves in Dean's.

★ A month before *Rebel Without a Cause* opened, Dean was killed in a car accident. He was only 24.

THE SEARCHERS

DIRECTOR: JOHN FORD

SCREENWRITER: FRANK S. NUGENT

WHAT IT'S ABOUT

It's 1868 and Ethan Edwards has just returned from the Civil War, and he is living at his brother's ranch in Texas. As he's out one day looking for lost cattle, Comanche Indians attack the ranch, killing his brother and his brother's wife, Martha (whom Ethan secretly loved), and taking the couple's two daughters—Lucy, the older one, and Debbie, a young girl. A posse that includes Ethan's nephew Martin (who is one-eighth Indian himself) and Lucy's sweetheart, Brad, takes off in search of the girls. When Ethan discovers Lucy's body near a group of Indians, Brad goes to seek revenge on the tribe and is killed.

After two years, Ethan and Martin return to the ranch for one night, and Ethan finds a clue that may lead to where Debbie is. Ethan leaves to investigate, and Martin heads off after him, convinced Ethan may kill Debbie if he finds her married to an Indian chief. The men continue to follow one lead after another until they finally find Scar, the chief they have been looking for, and Debbie, who *has* become one of his wives. But the Indians escape, and when Ethan and Martin find them again, Ethan gets to Debbie before Martin can. After years of looking for her, Ethan picks up Debbie and rather than killing her decides to bring her home.

The Searchers is based on Alan Le May's 1954 novel by the same name.

Who's In It

John Wayne as
Ethan Edwards

Jeffrey Hunter as
Martin Pawley

Vera Miles as
Laurie Jorgensen

Natalie Wood as
Debbie Edwards

Harry Carey Jr. as
Brad Jorgenson

Ward Bond as
Reverend Samuel
Johnston Clayton

Henry Brandon as
Chief Cicatrice

More With John Wayne

*She Wore a Yellow
Ribbon* (1949)
Rio Grande (1950)
Rio Bravo (1959)
*The Man Who Shot Liberty
Valance* (1962)

WHY ALL THE FUSS?

The Searchers is a definitive Western and represents one of the finest examples of the American-invented genre. It not only paved the way for movies like *Dances With Wolves*, *Unforgiven*, and *3:10 to Yuma*, but also opened the doors for new interpretations of the classic Western such as *Blazing Saddles* and *Brokeback Mountain*.

The movie features incredible imagery of the landscape of the West, with big, open shots of the sky, orange sunsets, and red rock formations, all of which highlight the overwhelming nature of the desert frontier, especially when it is contrasted with the very small silhouettes of the people inhabiting it.

Many consider this John Wayne's best performance. He plays a lone, brooding hero who is also a detestable and murderous racist. This contradiction is also thought to be one of the movie's many bits of brilliance.

The awesome soundtrack by Max Steiner is sweeping, epic, thunderous, and, yes, occasionally sappy.

Many major film directors (from Martin Scorsese to Steven Spielberg) cite *The Searchers* as a favorite film. You can see its influence in later "quest" movies like *Star Wars*, *Forest Gump*, and *Apocalypse Now* (page 129).

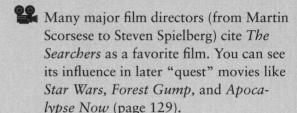

Bonus Material

★ A 1979 cover story in *New York Magazine* declared *The Searchers* the most influential movie in American history. Odd enough, it was never nominated for an Oscar.

★ George Lucas referenced this movie in *Star Wars: Episode IV* with the scene of Luke returning to his aunt and uncle's house to find it in flames—an homage to Martin returning to the ranch to find it and his foster family destroyed.

★ Spielberg says he has seen *The Searchers* perhaps a dozen times. References to the film can be seen in Spielberg's *Close Encounters of the Third Kind* in shots of the Western desert landscape and of a little boy lit from behind by orange light while standing in a doorway.

THE STUFF PEOPLE STILL TALK ABOUT

The rivalry shot: The search party rides in a valley, and a group of Indians rides parallel to them on a raised ridge. It is suspenseful and also shows how big the landscape is.

The doorway shots: The director dramatically frames Ethan's arrival, the final shot of Ethan alone after Debbie has returned, and many others in the doorway of the ranch.

The Ethan and Debbie reunion scene: Ethan finally finds Debbie, and in a tense moment it's unclear whether he's going to kill her.

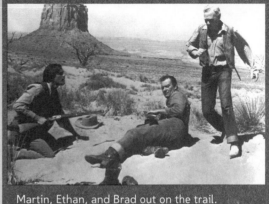

Martin, Ethan, and Brad out on the trail.

QUOTABLES

"That'll be the day."

Ethan says this repeatedly throughout the film—it's his catchphrase.
(This line inspired a famous Buddy Holly song, which got its title from the quote.)

"So we'll find 'em in the end, I promise you. We'll find 'em. Just as sure as the turnin' of the earth."

Ethan tells Martin this as they talk about finding Debbie.

"What do you want me to do? Draw you a picture? Spell it out? Don't ever ask me! Long as you live, don't ever ask me more."

Ethan says this to Brad after he's found Lucy dead and, most likely, raped.

1957

12 ANGRY MEN

DIRECTOR: SIDNEY LUMET

SCREENWRITER: REGINALD ROSE

WHAT IT'S ABOUT

A young ethnic-looking man (we never know his race or nationality) is on trial for murder, and a jury of 12 men is charged with deciding his fate—whether he lives or dies. After brief remarks from the judge, the dozen men retire to the jury room to deliberate; an initial poll produces an 11 to 1 decision, with only Juror #8 voting not guilty. With his hesitation based on the idea that any reasonable doubt should lead to an innocent verdict, Juror #8 persuades the men to reconsider the evidence.

While deliberating, the men debate the reliability of the eyewitnesses, the believability of the accused man's story, and even re-create the stabbing. The varied personalities and backgrounds of jurors also surface: One is meek, one is intensely logical, one grew up in a rough neighborhood, and yet another changes his vote just so he can go home. After a long, hot day filled with arguments, debates, personal revelations, and many additional votes, the 11 men who first voted guilty change their minds.

12 Angry Men **is based on Reginald Rose's 1954 television play by the same name.**

Who's In It

Henry Fonda as Juror #8

Martin Balsam as Juror #1

John Fiedler as Juror #2

Lee J. Cobb as Juror #3

E. G. Marshall as Juror #4

Jack Klugman as Juror #5

Edward Binns as Juror #6

Jack Warden as Juror #7

Joseph Sweeney as Juror #9

Ed Begley as Juror #10

George Voskovec as Juror #11

Robert Webber as Juror #12

More With Henry Fonda

Young Mr. Lincoln (1939)
The Grapes of Wrath (1940)
On Golden Pond (1981)

WHY ALL THE FUSS?

It is the granddaddy of all courtroom dramas, even though very little takes place in the courtroom. In fact, practically all court or police dramas, from *Law & Order* to *Boston Legal* to any *CSI*, have been influenced by this movie, in which the men of the jury debate motives, re-create witness testimony, and challenge each other's assumptions.

Noted for its dramatic performances, powerful direction, and tight script, the film was nominated for Best Picture, Best Director, and Best Screenplay (though it won no awards).

It's a very American movie, based on one of our country's main ideals: that all people are innocent until proven guilty. It also powerfully addresses issues such as prejudice, the assumptions people make about each other, and human nature in general.

It was unusual to base an entire movie in one room—and yet *12 Angry Men* is never boring.

Bonus Material

★ To make the movie feel increasingly claustrophobic, director Sidney Lumet shot the first third of the movie above eye level, the second third at eye level, and the last third below eye level, which created the effect of the room closing in around the men as the day wore on.

★ Henry Fonda was the only major movie star in the film; the rest of the performers were accomplished New York stage actors.

★ The movie is based on a play that was televised live on CBS in 1954; the tape of that performance was thought to be lost until 2003, when a copy was discovered.

★ In 1997, the movie was made for television again, with a cast that included James Gandolfini (*The Sopranos*), Jack Lemmon, William Petersen (*CSI*), and Tony Danza (*Taxi* and *Who's the Boss*).

THE STUFF PEOPLE STILL TALK ABOUT

Juror #8 (Henry Fonda, center) listens to the men discuss the case.

The racist rant scene: One juror passionately offers some thoughts on the case that clearly reveals he is a racist. He goes on for several minutes, and his fellow jurors, who are disgusted, get up and walk away from the table one by one.

Fonda's performance: He is the compassionate and measured juror who slowly persuades the other men to carefully consider the evidence before quickly sentencing the man on trial to death.

QUOTABLES

Juror #8: "I just want to talk."
Juror #7: "Well, what's there to talk about? Eleven men in here think he's guilty. No one had to think about it twice except you."

The beginning of a long day of deliberations.

1959 SOME LIKE IT HOT

DIRECTOR: BILLY WILDER

SCREENWRITERS: I.A.L. DIAMOND AND BILLY WILDER

WHAT IT'S ABOUT

Desperate to get out of town after witnessing a massive mob hit in Chicago, jazz musicians Joe and Jerry join a touring all-girl band. Of course, the only way they can do this is by dressing as girls. Joe becomes Josephine, and Jerry becomes Daphne, and they head out with their new band to a hotel in Florida for a gig. Joe falls hard for the sexy lead singer of the group, Sugar Kane Kowalczyk, and creates yet another persona, of a millionaire, in an attempt to woo her. Meanwhile, "Daphne" attracts the persistent attention of a real millionaire and must fend off his advances.

Later, the mobsters coincidentally show up at the hotel for a convention, and when they spot Joe and Jerry, they are intent on killing the pair. But a rival gangster takes out Joe and Jerry's would-be killers before Joe and Jerry are harmed. In the end, Sugar and Joe find love (even though at that point she knows he's not a millionaire). Jerry finally discloses his male identity to the millionaire who's been wooing him, but the rich guy just says, "Well, nobody's perfect!"

Who's In It

Jack Lemmon as
Jerry/Daphne

Tony Curtis as
Joe/Josephine

Marilyn Monroe as
Sugar Kane Kowalczyk

George Raft as
Spats Colombo

Joe E. Brown as
Osgood Fielding III

More With Marilyn Monroe

Gentlemen Prefer Blondes (1953)
The Seven Year Itch (1955)
Bus Stop (1956)
The Misfits (1961)

WHY ALL THE FUSS?

Jack Lemmon and Tony Curtis worked in drag way before anyone else. (*Tootsie* and *Mrs. Doubtfire* are direct descendents of this movie.)

Marilyn Monroe is gorgeous and compelling on screen, and she sings in the movie. Her songs include "I'm Through With Love" and "Runnin' Wild."

In 2000, the American Film Institute rated it as the number 1 comedy movie ever.

It is considered to be Monroe's finest work; she won a Golden Globe Award for her performance.

The comic timing of the three leads is considered impeccable, demonstrated in slapstick moments, double-takes, and expert delivery of the witty script.

QUOTABLES

"Story of my life. I always get the fuzzy end of the lollipop."
Sugar opens up to Daphne and Josephine with this odd but effective expression.

"Look at that! Look how she moves! It's like Jell-O on springs!"
Jerry comments to Joe as he watches Sugar (Monroe), with her amazing womanly curves, walk by them in the train station.

"Well, nobody's perfect!"
In the last line of the movie, millionaire Osgood responds after Jerry tells him that he's a man.

THE STUFF PEOPLE STILL TALK ABOUT

Curtis' spoof on Cary Grant: To inspire his fake millionaire character, Curtis used a hilarious, exaggerated version of suave movie star Cary Grant (see page 10 for more on Grant).

The dance scene: Daphne is being romanced by her millionaire suitor on a dance floor, and by the end she's shaking maracas and he has a flower in his mouth.

"I Wanna Be Loved by You": Monroe is super sexy in a barely there dress as she sings this playful song with the band.

★ Fashion designer Orry-Kelly created the costumes for Curtis, Lemmon, and Monroe. His work won the Academy Award for Best Costume Design.

★ A female impersonator was hired to give Curtis and Lemmon tips on how to convincingly play women.

★ The famous final line (see Quotables) was written the night before shooting finished.

Sugar and "Daphne" race back from the beach to tell "Josephine" about the handsome millionaire Sugar just met.

PSYCHO

DIRECTOR: ALFRED HITCHCOCK

SCREENWRITER: JOSEPH STEFANO

WHAT IT'S ABOUT

Marion Crane, an office worker at a Phoenix real estate firm, steals $40,000 from her job hoping that she can run away with her lover, Sam, who's deeply in debt to his ex-wife. She drives out of town but gets caught in a rainstorm one night and pulls over to the roadside Bates Motel, where she meets its nice—if not a little bit odd—caretaker, Norman, who lives there with his possessive mother. Being friendly, Norman invites Marion to eat dinner with him in the motel office, and Norman's mother is not happy about it. That night, while taking a shower, Marion is coincidentally stabbed to death by an older woman (though we can't see the killer's face). Later on, Norman discovers Marion's corpse and is horrified. He thinks this is the work of his jealous mom, and he meticulously gets rid of all evidence of the murder.

But that $40,000 is still missing from Marion's work, and an insurance investigator, Milton Arbogast, eventually ends up at the motel, looking for Marion and the money. Soon, the investigator's dead, too, and Sam, along with Marion's sister Lila, call the local police, who inform them that Mrs. Bates died many years ago. Sam and Lila eventually get to the bottom of things, and it's revealed that Norman suffers from multiple personality disorder and one of his personalities is his mother. So, he's been dressing up and killing people as her.

Who's In It

Anthony Perkins as
Norman Bates

Janet Leigh as
Marion Crane

Vera Miles as
Lila Crane

John Gavin as
Sam Loomis

Martin Balsam as
Milton Arbogast

More With Janet Leigh

Touch of Evil (1958)
The Manchurian Candidate
(1962)

WHY ALL THE FUSS?

Alfred Hitchcock's choice to kill off his main character (Marion) a third of the way into the film was groundbreaking. You just didn't do that back then.

Psycho has one of the most famous murder scenes of all time: the shower scene.

Psycho broke from the horror movie tradition of casting monsters as villains and instead made a mentally ill man the source of evil. Later films with this theme include *The Silence of the Lambs* (page 163), *Misery*, and *Single White Female*.

Bonus Material

★ Hitchcock insisted that no audience members be admitted to the movie theater after *Psycho's* opening credits, in part to make sure people became invested in the main character of Marion—and therefore be shocked by her murder. The movie was marketed with the line "See it from the beginning!"

★ Hitchcock wanted *Psycho* to look like a cheap horror movie, so he shot it in black and white (color was available, so it was an intentional choice) and used his lower-budget television show crew as opposed to the staff that worked on his more expensively made films.

★ Hitchcock's trademark appearance in his own film is in a scene at Marion's office—he's standing outside the window and wearing a cowboy hat. See *Rear Window* on page 31 to find out where he appeared in that film.

★ *The Simpsons* has spoofed *Psycho* a few times, referencing the famous shower scene and, through Principal Skinner's character, Norman Bates' twisted relationship with his mother.

THE STUFF PEOPLE STILL TALK ABOUT

The shower scene: Considered particularly brutal at the time, this famous sequence is noted for its total lack of dialogue and the fact that although it is bloody and violent, the audience never sees the knife enter Marion's flesh. Adding to it all is an unsettling, screeching soundtrack. (The editing, featuring close-ups and quick cuts, is also considered masterful.) Although mild by today's standards, the nudity of the shower scene was also quite racy back then.

Bernard Herrmann's disturbing score: It featured high-pitched, screeching violins.

Anthony Perkins' portrayal of Norman Bates: He's mild-mannered but also evasive, nervous, and creepy, in large part because he seems to be trying so hard to seem normal.

Marion is attacked in the famous shower scene.

QUOTABLES

"A boy's best friend is his mother."
Norman says this to Marion as they eat dinner. (Apparently so, for Norman.)

"Mother! Oh God, mother! Blood! Blood!"
Norman, offscreen to his mother, reacting to the killing of Marion.

"We all go a little mad sometimes."
Norman tells Marion this in defense of his mom after Marion suggests institutionalizing her.

BREAKFAST AT TIFFANY'S
DIRECTOR: BLAKE EDWARDS
SCREENWRITER: GEORGE AXELROD

WHAT IT'S ABOUT

Breakfast at Tiffany's tells the story of 1950s Manhattan party girl and socialite Holly Golightly and her relationship with neighbor Paul Varjak, a hot, struggling young writer. Holly and Paul bond over the fact that they are both being funded by rich benefactors—in her case, several wealthy sugar daddies and, in his case, an older woman referred to as 2-E (for Emily Eustace).

Paul struggles with writer's block and tries to win Holly's affection, but when Holly's former husband—whom she married when she was 14—shows up, her small-town past is exposed and, with that, comes complications. Her jail visits to Sally Tomato, a mob boss for whom she's unwittingly helping to relay messages (in return for some cash), wreak further havoc. Determined to marry rich (her first marriage was annulled), Holly sets her sights on more than one wealthy man, but in the end, she is convinced by a really ticked off and frustrated Paul that he is who she really belongs with.

Breakfast at Tiffany's is based on Truman Capote's 1958 novella of the same name.

Who's In It

Audrey Hepburn as
Holly Golightly

George Peppard as
Paul Varjak

Patricia Neal as 2-E

Mickey Rooney as
Mr. Yunioshi

More With Audrey Hepburn

Roman Holiday (1953)
Sabrina (1954)
The Children's Hour (1961)
My Fair Lady (1964)

WHY ALL THE FUSS?

Audrey Hepburn created a style icon with her character. The modern-day actress most frequently compared to Hepburn is Natalie Portman, but no one has ever been able to rival the elegance of Hepburn.

The opening scene is one of cinema's and pop culture's classic images. In it, Holly peers into the window of Tiffany's, elegantly sporting pearls, a simple black dress, sunglasses, and upswept, frosted hair. The dress she is wearing has since become a known style: LBD, or "little black dress."

The movie's music was also a part of its success; Henry Mancini's score won an Academy Award and included the now famous song "Moon River." Hepburn got lots of praise for her rendition of the song, which Holly sings while sitting on her windowsill.

People still love *Breakfast at Tiffany's* because they easily relate to Holly's mad escapades, her late nights partying and boozing, and the life of a charming and vulnerable twentysomething girl who's living on the edge in Manhattan. She is most definitely a precursor to *Sex & the City's* Carrie Bradshaw.

Breakfast at Tiffany's also influenced the TV show *Gossip Girl.* In the episode "Bad News Blair," the character Blair dreams that she is Holly in a reenactment of a scene from the film.

Bonus Material

★ Truman Capote originally wanted Marilyn Monroe for the role of Holly Golightly, but studio executives overruled him and cast Hepburn instead.

★ Hepburn's iconic wardrobe for the film was designed by the French luxury label, Givenchy.

★ The real name of the cat in the film was Putney.

THE STUFF PEOPLE STILL TALK ABOUT

The party scene: Holly holds a wild, wild party in her small apartment. It's cramped, people get drunk, and the cops eventually break up the bash.

Holly's cat, named "Cat": At the end of the movie, she loses him and dramatically searches for him in the rain with Paul. She finds her cat and accepts what is basically a marriage proposal from Paul with a passionate kiss.

Mr. Yunioshi: The portrayal of Japanese landlord Mr. Yunioshi by Caucasian actor Mickey Rooney is cartoonish, and now considered somewhat racist and offensive.

Glamour girl Holly smoking a cigarette in her little black dress.

QUOTABLES

"I'll never let anybody put me in a cage."

Holly says this to Paul after he has declared his love for her; she loves him, too, but is afraid of getting close to anyone.

"You know what's wrong with you, Miss Whoever you are?"

The first line of Paul's angry speech, in which he calls Holly a coward because she's afraid to fall in love.

51

WEST SIDE STORY

DIRECTORS: JEROME ROBBINS AND ROBERT WISE

SCREENWRITERS: JEROME ROBBINS AND ERNEST LEHMAN

WHAT IT'S ABOUT

West Side Story started as a Broadway musical that was an updated, 1950s New York take on Shakespeare's *Romeo and Juliet*. The musical was about two lovers from different ethnicities, and the movie was modeled after it.

Two rival gangs, the Puerto Rican Sharks and the Polish Jets, are at war. Tony, a former Jet, meets Maria, the sister of the top dog of the Sharks. Against a colorful, urban backdrop the two fall in love. Their forbidden romance blossoms, and they plan to run away together, but the tensions between the two gangs increase, and a final showdown is scheduled. Tony and Maria become tragically caught up in the street war, and Tony is killed. All of the movie's action—from a high school dance to gang meetings to romantic interludes—is expressed in intricately choreographed dance numbers to pop and romantic show tunes.

Who's In It

Natalie Wood as
Maria

Richard Beymer as
Tony

Russ Tamblyn as
Riff

Rita Moreno as
Anita

George Chakiris as
Bernardo

More With Natalie Wood

Rebel Without a Cause
(1955, page 34)
The Searchers (1956,
page 37)
Splendor in the Grass (1961)
Gypsy (1962)

Bonus Material

★ **Both Elvis Presley and Warren Beatty were considered for the role of Tony, but it ultimately went to Richard Beymer, who, many people felt, was not a great choice. It also seemed a bit of a stretch putting major star Natalie Wood in the role of Maria because she wasn't the least bit Latin.**

WHY ALL THE FUSS?

The songs of Leonard Bernstein and Stephen Sondheim are spectacular; they're catchy, moving, beautiful, romantic, and have great lyrics. Classic tunes from the movie include "Jet Song," "I Feel Pretty," "Tonight," and "Maria."

The choreography by codirector Jerome Robbins was revolutionary at the time for its unconventional nature. He was able to make a whole bunch of singing and dancing boys look cool and tough while dancing their way through a rumble.

Rita Moreno as Anita was awesome. She later went on to be in things like *The Electric Company*, *Law & Order*, and *Ugly Betty*.

West Side Story was awarded 10 Oscars, including Best Picture and Best Director.

Bernardo (center) and the Sharks in a rumble dance scene.

QUOTABLES

"When you're a Jet, you're a Jet all the way, from your first cigarette to your last dyin' days."

Riff sings this to his fellow Jets, illustrating the bonds of brotherhood formed inside the gang.

"I like to be in America."

Anita sings this in "America," as she explains why she's glad to be in the United States, as opposed to her homeland of Puerto Rico.

THE STUFF PEOPLE STILL TALK ABOUT

"America": Moreno almost steals the movie in this number, which speaks to the immigrant experience in the United States, and points out that living in the US often provides more freedoms for immigrant women than living in their homelands does.

"Maria": The romantic love song that Tony sings after meeting Maria.

"Gee, Officer Krupke!": The Jets sing this satirical number to mock the police and the supposed reasons they are juvenile delinquents (bad neighborhoods, bad parents). The final lyric in the song is "Gee, Officer Krupke, Krup you!"

The dubbed singing: Wood's singing was dubbed by Marni Nixon, and Jim Bryant sang Beymer's numbers. Today this would rarely happen—in musicals, actors are expected, hired, and trained to sing their own parts.

The finger-snapping fight scene: *West Side Story*'s gang rumble has been parodied in modern pop culture lots of times. One classic example is the fight scene between the news teams in the movie *Anchorman*, in which everything from the background music to the drawn switchblade is reminiscent of the Jets vs. Sharks.

Bonus Material

★ The actors playing the rival gang members were encouraged to pull pranks on each other to fuel the spirit of competition.

★ Robert Wise and Jerome Robbins were the first codirectors to receive an Academy Award. Due to bitter infighting on the set, neither thanked the other when accepting the award.

★ Wise was the film editor on the landmark movie *Citizen Kane* (page 17).

1967

THE GRADUATE

DIRECTOR: MIKE NICHOLS

SCREENWRITERS: BUCK HENRY AND CALDER WILLINGHAM

WHAT IT'S ABOUT

Benjamin Braddock just graduated from college and is anxious about his future. At a graduation party that his parents throw, his dad's law partner's wife, Mrs. Robinson, asks him for a ride home. Once there, she tries to get it on with Ben, taking him up to a bedroom and removing her clothes. Weirded out, he takes off—but a few days later, he calls her and the two start having a secret affair.

When he's not sleeping with Mrs. Robinson (an act the audience never actually sees), Ben just lays around the house and on a raft in the pool, depressed. His parents get tired of his laziness, and they pressure him to apply to grad school and to go out with Elaine—the Robinsons' daughter—while she is home on break from UC Berkeley. He finally takes Elaine on a date and falls for her, despite the fact that he had promised Mrs. Robinson he would never date her daughter. Jealous and outraged, Mrs. Robinson threatens to expose the affair, and so Ben tells Elaine himself. The Robinsons' marriage is now in turmoil, and Elaine won't speak to Ben, either. She goes back to school, where she meets someone else and gets engaged, but Ben becomes obsessed and dramatically interrupts Elaine's wedding. All hell breaks loose, but Ben and Elaine escape the scene and hop on a city bus heading nowhere in particular.

The Graduate is based on Charles Webb's 1963 novel by the same name.

Who's In It

Dustin Hoffman as Benjamin Braddock

Anne Bancroft as Mrs. Robinson

Katharine Ross as Elaine Robinson

William Daniels as Mr. Braddock

Murray Hamilton as Mr. Robinson

Elizabeth Wilson as Mrs. Braddock

More Directed by Mike Nichols

Who's Afraid of Virginia Woolf? (1966)
Catch-22 (1970)
Silkwood (1983)
Working Girl (1988)

More With Anne Bancroft

The Miracle Worker (1962)
The Turning Point (1977)
Agnes of God (1985)

WHY ALL THE FUSS?

The Graduate gave voice to a whole generation of kids who felt lost after graduating college.

Ben's rebellion against doing what he was supposed to do (get a job, get married) after college, and his affair with an older, married woman (quite shocking at the time) hit home for anyone who was rejecting traditional middle-class values.

Dustin Hoffman's performance as Ben, a hot young guy in the midst of an existential crisis, made him a major movie star.

The Graduate set the stage for films that featured an older woman and a younger man like *American Pie*, *White Palace*, *Tadpole*, *The Reader*, and *Class*.

Anne Bancroft as the middle-aged and complicated Mrs. Robinson showed audiences that older ladies still have major sex appeal. Bancroft's character was also a response to the "wholesome suburban mom" icon that became such a fixture in the '50s and '60s.

The Simon & Garfunkel soundtrack, featuring "Sound of Silence" and "Mrs. Robinson" became a huge hit. "Mrs. Robinson" was remade in the '90s by the Lemonheads, and that version also appeared in *American Pie 2*, during a similar situation.

QUOTABLES

"Plastics."

A family friend says this to an obviously puzzled and overwhelmed Ben on what career path he should take. It's supposedly the wave of the future and a ticket to security, but also sounds like the most boring thing in the world.

"Mrs. Robinson, you're trying to seduce me....aren't you?"

A very uncomfortable Ben says this to Mrs. Robinson, as she is most definitely trying to seduce him.

THE STUFF PEOPLE STILL TALK ABOUT

The sexy leg shots: Standing in the living room of the Robinson's house, Benjamin is framed by Mrs. Robinson's bent leg as she's trying to seduce him. In another similar image, Benjamin stands in the background as Mrs. Robinson's sexy stockinged leg sticks out in the frame.

The drifting scene: Ben is drifting in the pool, very actively doing nothing, backed by "Sound of Silence."

The wedding scene: At the end of the movie, Ben interrupts Elaine's wedding by yelling her name through a plate glass window, and they escape on a city bus. (This has been parodied many times, including in *Wayne's World 2* and in an episode of *The Simpsons*.)

Mrs. Robinson and Ben in bed together.

Bonus Material

★ Even though they were supposed to be a whole generation apart, Hoffman was 30 and Bancroft was only 36 at the time of filming. Hoffman looked naturally young, and makeup and lighting were used to make Anne Bancroft look older.

★ Plain White Ts' music video "Our Time Now" is a direct reference to *The Graduate* and includes several reenactments of scenes from the movie.

★ The original title of the song "Mrs. Robinson" was "Mrs. Roosevelt," but Simon & Garfunkel changed it upon Nichols' request, when he wanted to use the song (which had been written, but not recorded yet) for the movie.

★ The birthday party scene in the movie *Old School* shows Will Ferrell's character shooting himself in the neck with a tranquilizer gun and falling into the pool while "Sound of Silence" plays in the background.

1967

BONNIE AND CLYDE

DIRECTOR: ARTHUS PENN

SCREENWRITERS: DAVID NEWMAN AND ROBERT BENTON

WHAT IT'S ABOUT

Bonnie and Clyde is based on the story of real-life Depression-era bank robbers Clyde Barrow and Bonnie Parker. Bonnie, a small-town waitress with big dreams spots Clyde eyeing her mother's car from her bedroom window. She goes downstairs to confront him and is immediately struck by his charm. Before you know it, Bonnie and the ex-con are riding around in stolen cars and holding up banks at gunpoint. They pick up three partners along the way—a half-baked mechanic and Clyde's brother and his whiny wife—and the thieves find themselves on an increasingly violent crime spree across the country.

Still, they stick together, and when a Texan ranger tries to take them down during a roadside pit stop, the gang humiliates him by photographing the ranger, handcuffed, with Bonnie kissing him—and submitting the photos to the media. Eventually, the "Barrow Gang" becomes famous and the cops (especially the Texan one, who they don't kill) won't rest until they are captured. Throughout, Bonnie and Clyde's relationship is passionate but frustrated by the fact that Clyde has performance anxiety (in the sack). He eventually gets his act together, but soon after, the doomed lovers meet their end in a violent rain of bullets.

Who's In It

Warren Beatty as
Clyde Barrow

Faye Dunaway as
Bonnie Parker

Michael J. Pollard as
C. W. Moss

Estelle Parsons as
Blanche

Gene Hackman as
Buck Barrow

More With
Warren Beatty

Splendor in the Grass (1961)
Shampoo (1975)
Reds (1981)
Bugsy (1991)

More With
Faye Dunaway

The Thomas Crown Affair (1968)
Chinatown (1974)
Three Days of the Condor (1975)
Network (1976, page 106)
Mommie Dearest (1981)

WHY ALL THE FUSS?

The movie presented its violent, outlaw main characters as likable heroes. These kinds of characters later became known as "anti-heroes."

Released at a time when the country was engaged in a culture war that pitted the establishment against a youth movement (think: Vietnam protests, the Civil Rights movement), *Bonnie and Clyde* spoke to a younger, anti-establishment America.

Many audience members and critics found the violence—which was presented in an appealing, sometimes beautiful way—to be appalling. The fact that the film was often funny, had a jingling banjo-driven soundtrack, and made Bonnie and Clyde's story seem like a fun adventure didn't help matters.

Both in style and attitude, *Bonnie and Clyde* paved the way for landmark movies of the '70s such as *Easy Rider* (page 70) and *The Godfather* (page 87), as well as more recent films including *Fight Club*, *Reservoir Dogs*, *Natural Born Killers*, and *Thelma & Louise*.

Clyde and Bonnie in a heated gunfight.

Bonus Material

★ The movie got panned at first for its casual treatment of violence, but Warren Beatty persuaded the studio to re-release the film later that year, and it received new, positive press. By December 1968, *Time* published the story "The New Cinema: Violence…Sex…Art" with Faye Dunaway and Warren Beatty as Bonnie and Clyde on the cover.

★ Elvis Presley, Jay Z and Beyonce, PJ Harvey, and Toni Braxton have all made songs that reference the renegade love affair of Bonnie and Clyde.

THE STUFF PEOPLE STILL TALK ABOUT

The clothes: Beatty's double-breasted suits and Faye Dunaway's 1930s outfits and signature beret became fashion trends after the film's release.

The overall cinematography style: Intending to create an American take on the French new wave movement of filmmaking, the producers used techniques of that form, including fast cuts and narrow establishing shots that did not give an immediately clear idea of what was going on.

Clyde's impotence: Clyde, who was played by then hunky screen idol Beatty, is unable to perform sexually throughout most of the movie. While there is some research that shows that Clyde may have been bisexual, making him impotent was entirely a directorial choice not based on historical fact.

The shoot-out scene: The movie concludes with an unforgettable, slow-motion showdown between the police and the duo—it's very loud, and lots of bullets fly.

QUOTABLES

"I ain't much of a lover boy."

Clyde brushes off Bonnie at the beginning of the movie when she makes a sexual advance toward him.

"We rob banks."

Clyde describes his profession to a pair of farmers who have lost their homes. He's very friendly and charming about it—not exactly what you would expect from a dangerous criminal.

1968

PLANET OF THE APES

DIRECTOR: FRANKLIN J. SHAFFNER

SCREENWRITERS: MICHAEL WILSON AND ROD SERLING

WHAT IT'S ABOUT

A crew of four astronauts from Earth crash-lands in a lake on a mysterious planet that the group's leader, George Taylor (known as Taylor), guesses is 320 light-years from Earth. (He also believes they are in the year 3978, having taken a look at the ship's time reading.) In this primitive, desertlike world, apes rule and humans are enslaved, mute savages.

Taylor and a group of humans are captured and enslaved by the local apes, and one of them, Zira, a chimpanzee psychologist dedicated to understanding human behavior, takes a special interest in Taylor. She sees that he is intelligent and thinks he may be a missing link between the mute humans on the planet and the evolved apes. But lead ape Dr. Zaius is set on keeping Taylor captive, and Zira and her fiancé, Cornelius, help him break out of the cage where he's being kept. Along with Nova, a pretty human mute, they head to the Forbidden Zone, where there is evidence of an advanced civilization of non-simians, but Zaius arrives to end the party. Taylor defeats Zaius, and he takes off with food, water, and Nova in search of a life with her far from the apes, but instead comes upon an alarming site: the Statue of Liberty is sticking out of the beach. It is then that he realizes he's landed on Earth—and that human civilization had been wiped out by nuclear weapons many years before.

Who's In It

Charlton Heston as George Taylor

Roddy McDowall as Cornelius

Kim Hunter as Zira

Maurice Evans as Dr. Zaius

Linda Harrison as Nova

More With Charlton Heston

The Ten Commandments (1956)
Ben-Hur (1959)
El Cid (1961)
The Agony and the Ecstasy (1965)

More Written by Rod Serling

The Twilight Zone TV series (1959-1964)

Planet of the Apes is based on the 1963 Pierre Boulle French novel *La Planete des Singes*.

WHY ALL THE FUSS?

Planet of the Apes convincingly and cleverly depicts an upside-down society in which humans are animals and apes are civilized. The apes keep humans in cages, put them on leashes, experiment on them, and say condescending things like "Human see, human do" and "To apes, all men look alike." It's a commentary on the hierarchy of our society, questioning humans' treatment of those species it deems less intelligent and more savage.

Makeup supervisor John Chambers is given much of the credit for the movie's success—his latex ape masks made the simian characters believable, not laughable. He received an honorary Oscar for outstanding makeup achievement for his work on the film.

It contains one of the most famous twist endings in film history.

The movie spawned four sequels, a television series, tons of related merchandise (dolls, lunchboxes), and was remade by Tim Burton in 2001 with Mark Wahlberg in the lead role.

Bonus Material

★ The initial screenplay for the movie featured a more technologically advanced group of apes, which is how the novel had depicted the society. However, budget concerns forced producers to create a society that was more primitive (the apes rode on horses instead of in flying machines).

★ Makeup master Chambers was a World War II veteran who had worked with prosthetics in the military and moved to Hollywood to apply his skill there. He also created Mr. Spock's ears for the TV series *Star Trek*.

★ In order to convince the studio heads that a serious movie with talking apes could be made, the producers shot a scene from the script using an early version of the makeup. After seeing it, the studio gave the go-ahead.

THE STUFF PEOPLE STILL TALK ABOUT

Cornelius, Zira, and Lucius help Taylor and Nova escape and head for the Forbidden Zone.

Charlton Heston as action hero: The role of Taylor was very different from the ones Heston had played earlier in his career, such as Moses in *The Ten Commandments* and Judah Ben-Hur in *Ben-Hur*.

The ape appearance scene: When clothed, gun-toting apes ride in on horseback to violently round up herds of humans, it becomes clear that this is a different kind of planet.

The shot of the Statue of Liberty: It creates a twist ending that provides insight into everything that has come before.

QUOTABLES

"Take your stinking paws off me, you damned dirty ape!"

Taylor, who has escaped from his cage is captured by the apes, and shocks them all when he utters these first words to them.

"You maniacs! You blew it up! Ah, damn you. God damn you all to hell!"

Taylor exclaims this in the movie's final scene, when he realizes he's on Earth, and mankind's own savagery destroyed humankind and the planet as he once knew it.

1968

NIGHT OF THE LIVING DEAD

DIRECTOR: GEORGE A. ROMERO

SCREENWRITERS: GEORGE A. ROMERO AND JOHN A. RUSSO

WHAT IT'S ABOUT

Siblings Johnny and Barbra visit their dad's grave in a Pennsylvania small town, and for fun Johnny freaks Barbra out with some creepy cemetery humor. Next thing you know, a gaunt old guy attacks the pair, taking Johnny out; Barbra escapes to what looks like an abandoned farmhouse, only to find a rotting body.

Barbra runs away and then meets up with a guy named Ben, who fends off some approaching zombies by killing them with a golf club. They return to the house, where they discover a small group of people—two parents, their injured daughter, and a young couple—who have taken refuge there. A radio in the house airs news reports that mass murdering is happening all down the East Coast and the killers are eating the flesh of their victims.

Meanwhile, the group argues about the best strategy for staying alive, and more and more creatures—dazed, slow-moving, relentless zombies—encircle the house. Further news reports suggest that the radiation from a Venus satellite may be reanimating the recently dead and advise people to head to rescue stations. The group then devises a plan to fend off the zombies with fire and make a break for a nearby truck, but the plan goes horribly wrong when the truck catches fire and two people die. With zombies closing in on the house fast, the remaining survivors realize they must stay at the house and wait for help, but Ben is the only person who makes it through the night alive. It seems as if he might be saved when the cops show up in the morning, but they mistake Ben for a zombie and shoot him dead.

Who's In It

Duane Jones as Ben

Judith O'Dea as Barbra

Karl Hardman as
Harry Cooper

Marilyn Eastman as
Helen Cooper

Keith Wayne as Tom

Judith Ridley as
Judy

Kyra Schon as
Karen Cooper

WHY ALL THE FUSS?

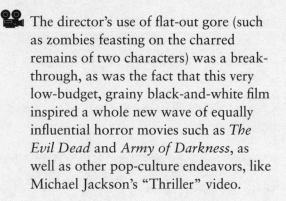

This indie movie, made for next to nothing, is still one of the scariest movies around, and with it Romero pretty much invented the zombie flick.

Without this movie, classic horror flicks of the '70s and '80s such as *The Texas Chainsaw Massacre, Halloween, Friday the 13th*, and *A Nightmare on Elm Street* would not exist—never mind the more recent crop of zombie movies that includes *28 Days Later, Shaun of the Dead*, and *28 Weeks Later*.

The director's use of flat-out gore (such as zombies feasting on the charred remains of two characters) was a breakthrough, as was the fact that this very low-budget, grainy black-and-white film inspired a whole new wave of equally influential horror movies such as *The Evil Dead* and *Army of Darkness*, as well as other pop-culture endeavors, like Michael Jackson's "Thriller" video.

QUOTABLES

"They're coming to get you, Barbra!"

Johnny jokingly says this to Barbra in the cemetery, but the line foretells the horror to come.

THE STUFF PEOPLE STILL TALK ABOUT

The garden trowel scene: A daughter, who has become a zombie herself, brutally kills her mother with a garden trowel. It's gory and harsh.

Cannibal lunch: The zombies eat the charred remains of victims after a truck has exploded.

Creepy zombies stage an attack.

★ George Romero made the film for about $100,000, which was considered ridiculously cheap even back then.

★ Despite the fact that *Night of the Living Dead* is considered one of the most influential movies in film history (in 1999, the Library of Congress acknowledged its historical importance), the director made very little money from it because of a copyright technicality.

★ The *South Park* episode "Night of the Living Homeless" is a direct reference and features funny references to the film throughout the episode.

1968

2001: A SPACE ODYSSEY

DIRECTOR: STANLEY KUBRICK

SCREENWRITERS: STANLEY KUBRICK AND ARTHUR C. CLARKE

WHAT IT'S ABOUT

Somewhat defying traditional plot explanation, this nonlinear movie starts in prehistory, with long scenes of apes eating, sleeping, and hanging out. Then, a mysterious monolith (a big, black rectangular slab) appears to two rival groups of apes. Soon after, one primate discovers a skeleton of another animal and then uses that bone to kill another ape. The sense is that the monolith triggered an important evolutionary leap: the ability to use weapons.

Then, suddenly, it's 2001, and a scientist is headed to a space station orbiting Earth to participate in a mission to the moon, where another monolith has shown up. Eighteen months later, another crew is sent to Jupiter, where other monolith activity has been detected. Among this crew are five men guided by one highly advanced supercomputer named HAL 9000. Three of the men are temporarily frozen in hibernation until the spaceship arrives at Jupiter. But HAL starts to misbehave, and when he gets wind that the two awake astronauts (Dave Bowman and Frank Poole) are considering disconnecting him, he kills everyone except Dave, who defeats HAL by unplugging all of his circuits. HAL slowly dies, while saying very human things like, "I'm afraid, Dave."

Dave is now still in space, and when he encounters another monolith in Jupiter's orbit, he is sucked into a tremendously colorful wormhole and somehow ends up in what looks like an 18th-century French apartment or hotel, in which he watches himself change into an old person. Finally, another monolith appears, and Dave becomes a giant "star baby" hovering over Earth.

Who's In It

Keir Dullea as
Dave Bowman

Gary Lockwood as
Frank Poole

William Sylvester as
Heywood Floyd

Doug Rain as
HAL 9000

2001: A Space Odyssey was inspired by Arthur C. Clarke's short story *The Sentinel.*

WHY ALL THE FUSS?

 If *2001* boggles your mind and you have no idea what it's about, don't worry—you're not alone. The movie is known for being somewhat incomprehensible, but it's also regarded as a breakthrough film that raises questions about evolution, man's relationship to technology, the destiny of the human race, and more.

 It's a sci-fi movie that doesn't include a lot of sci-fi movie elements. There are no fight sequences or big explosions, very little plot, and not a single alien. Instead, it has incredibly slow sequences of things moving through space to a classical soundtrack.

 It received Oscar nominations for Best Director, Best Screenplay, and Best Art Direction.

 The stunning special effects, all done without the use of computers, were mind-blowing then (they won the Oscar) and remain so.

Astronaut Frank Poole before HAL gets to him.

Bonus Material

★ Stanley Kubrick was behind in prepping the film for its North American premiere, but he had to make the trip from the UK to the US. Notoriously afraid of flying, he continued editing the movie on a transatlantic journey from the UK to the US aboard the luxury ship *The Queen Elizabeth*.

★ To create the futuristic computer screens in the movie, 35-millimeter movies were projected onto blank screens from behind.

THE STUFF PEOPLE STILL TALK ABOUT

The bone-to-spaceship cut: The film cuts directly from a bone thrown in the air by a primate to a spaceship floating above Earth.

The incredible, large-scale imagery: Images of the sun and the moon aligning directly over the monolith, the massive space station rotating in slow motion, and the iconic "star child" hovering over Earth in the film's final shot.

HAL: This menacing rebellious computer that has a cold, monotone voice is a symbol of advanced technology gone very wrong.

The HAL death scene: Dave Bowman disconnects HAL, and as he's doing so, HAL attempts to talk him out of it. It's both strange and sort of funny, because a computer is trying to bargain with a man that it was intent on killing.

The use of the classical music pieces: "Thus Spoke Zarathustra" by Richard Strauss and Johann Strauss' "Blue Danube Waltz" are not obvious choices for a sci-fi movie soundtrack, yet they are now strongly associated with the film.

QUOTABLES

"Open the pod bay doors, HAL."
Dave says this to HAL, who, in an act of rebellion, leaves the astronaut out in space to die. It's the moment when it's clear that HAL is trying to kill Dave and take over the ship.

"I'm sorry, Dave, I'm afraid I can't do that."
HAL's chilling response to Dave's above request.

1969

EASY RIDER

DIRECTOR: DENNIS HOPPER

SCREENWRITERS: PETER FONDA, DENNIS HOPPER, AND TERRY SOUTHERN

WHAT IT'S ABOUT

Wyatt (aka "Captain America") and Billy are two twentysomething hippie-type rebels who make some big money on a drug deal in LA and decide to ride their motorcycles to New Orleans for Mardi Gras. Wyatt is the cool, handsome one with leather pants and American flags painted all over his bike, jacket, and helmet; Billy is the more anxious, high-strung of the two, who always needs to get wasted and never seems content with anything.

With the cash stowed in Wyatt's gas tank, the two set out on a cross-country journey through states that don't always appreciate their long-haired, anti-establishment vibe. On their journey they hang out with hippies in a commune, land in jail from illegally marching in a parade, meet a young alcoholic lawyer (who comes along for the ride until being brutally killed one night by strangers), drop LSD in a cemetery with prostitutes, and sleep under the stars. Soon, the duo travels to Florida to "retire," but both are killed on the road by two hippie-hating rednecks with a shotgun.

Who's In It

Peter Fonda as Wyatt

Dennis Hopper as Billy

Jack Nicholson as George Hanson

Karen Black as Karen

Toni Basil as Mary

More With Dennis Hopper

Cool Hand Luke (1967)
Apocalypse Now (1979, page 129)
Blue Velvet (1986)
True Romance (1993)
Speed (1994)

Bonus Material

★ Much of the dialogue for the movie was improvised, and the actors were just as stoned as their characters throughout the film.

WHY ALL THE FUSS?

The movie debuted when a culture war was raging between the older establishment and the youth population. This movie—filled with sex, drugs, and rock 'n' roll—was seen as a statement made by the youth. For this reason, it is said to be the movie that "defined a generation."

Easy Rider was one of the first movies to bring alternative culture (in the form of hippies, communes, and pot-smoking rebels) to the big screen, and its rock 'n' roll soundtrack, scenic sequences of the open road, and Captain America's outfit—his motorcycle, helmet, and jacket all feature images of the American flag—are now a permanent fixture in the annals of pop culture.

The film won Dennis Hopper the award for Best First Film at the prestigious Cannes Film Festival and gave Jack Nicholson his breakout role.

The huge success of this alternative, low-budget film had long-lasting effects that ultimately led to young filmmakers like George Lucas, Steven Spielberg, and Brian DePalma getting a shot in Hollywood.

Captain America cruising the highway with George on the back.

Bonus Material

★ According to director Hopper, the movie was modeled after a Western: The character of Wyatt was named after Wyatt Earp, and Billy was a nod to Billy the Kid.

★ Actor Rip Torn was the first choice to play George the lawyer, but he turned down the role. Later, Nicholson was cast and received a Best Supporting Actor nomination for his performance.

THE STUFF PEOPLE STILL TALK ABOUT

"Born to Be Wild": Steppenwolf wrote the film's signature song.

The shots of the open road: As the two men cross the country, they see beautiful landscapes that encouraged a whole new wave of road trippers.

The soundtrack: The movie's songs by Steppenwolf, Jimi Hendrix, the Byrds, and others, have become legendary. (Ironically, this compilation of already released songs was only the result of Hopper not having enough money to hire someone to write new music for the film.)

The LSD trip scene: The two men do drugs in a cemetery with two prostitutes, and their experience is expressed through jarring images, editing, and sound.

The watch scene: Wyatt removes his watch and throws it on the ground—it's an act that represents his rejection of the establishment.

George's football helmet: George, the lawyer, is wearing a football helmet instead of a motorcycle helmet because that's all he has.

QUOTABLES

"It's real hard to be free when you're bought and sold in the marketplace."
George says this to Billy and Wyatt around a campfire, offering one of his anti-establishment musings.

"You know, Billy, we blew it."
Wyatt says this to Billy toward the end of the movie. We're not entirely sure what he means, but the sense is that he feels they failed somehow in their quest for freedom.

"If God did not exist, it would be necessary to invent him."
Wyatt says this to Billy, quoting the French writer Voltaire, after a few hours spent in a whorehouse in New Orleans, some days after George was killed.

GIMME SHELTER

DIRECTORS: ALBERT MAYSLES, DAVID MAYSLES, AND CHARLOTTE ZWERIN

WHAT IT'S ABOUT

Gimme Shelter is a documentary (or "rockumentary") following the last days of the Rolling Stones' 1969 US tour, as well as the notorious free concert at Altamont Speedway in California, at which a man was killed. The backdrop for the documentary is the end of the 1960s, an era of free love, peace movements, and recreational drug use that is thought by many to be symbolically punctuated by the dark events that happen in this film.

Gimme Shelter follows the band from a live performance of the Stones at a 1969 concert at Madison Square Garden to the various hotel rooms band members stayed in while on tour, through the planning of the massive free concert at Altamont, where they played with other bands like Ike and Tina Turner, Jefferson Airplane, and the Flying Burrito Brothers. The most famed footage in the documentary, though, is that of the killing of a young African-American man named Meredith Hunter at the hands of a member of the Hells Angels, a group of bikers who had been hired to work security for the event. It happens while the Rolling Stones are performing, the crowd is drugged-up and on edge, and dozens of people are crushed against the stage. Despite Jagger's attempts to calm the increasingly amped-up crowd, a scuffle occurs, and suddenly Hunter is being stabbed to death.

Who's In It

Mick Jagger
lead singer

Charlie Watts
drummer

Keith Richards
guitarist

Mick Taylor
guitarist

Bill Wyman
bassist

Melvin Belli
the Rolling Stones' lawyer

Sam Cutler
the Rolling Stones' tour manager

WHY ALL THE FUSS?

The movie is thought to capture the death of the 1960s, a decade noted for its peace-loving hippies and free-wheeling culture. The Altamont concert, which was modeled after the East Coast love fest that was Woodstock, was marked not by peace and love, but by violence, chaos, and death.

The film provides a look into the world of rock 'n' roll by documenting one of the biggest bands of all time as they perform, record in the studio, promote the upcoming concert, and deal with the aftermath of the tragic events.

Mick Jagger on stage at Altamont.

Bonus Material

★ Contrary to popular belief, the stabbing at Altamont did not occur during the performance of the Rolling Stones song "Gimme Shelter," but instead during "Under My Thumb."

★ Many people think that the lyrics "No angel born in hell/Could break that Satan's spell..." in Don McLean's epic song "American Pie" refer to Mick Jagger and the Altamont concert, although McLean famously refuses on principle to explain the tune's words.

★ George Lucas, who would go on to create *Star Wars*, was a cameraman on the film.

★ For their services, the Hells Angels had reportedly agreed on $500 worth of beer as payment.

THE STUFF PEOPLE STILL TALK ABOUT

Altamont: Altamont is now representative of a mass music gathering gone very wrong and is brought up whenever that happens. (For example, Woodstock '99, which was marked by fires, violence, and rape, was referred to as a new generation's Altamont.) If you want to see what Altamont was like, watch *Gimme Shelter*.

The replay of the murder scene: In the documentary, we see the Rolling Stones as they are editing the film of the Altamont concert. The moment when Meredith Hunter pulls a gun and is then stabbed is played back in slow motion by director Albert Maysles, and the band looks on, horrified.

The "Wild Horses" scene: The band is in the recording studio and is listening to a play-back of what would become one of its most famous songs. The filmmakers zoom in on the quiet, contemplative faces of Jagger and Watts, offering a different view of the wild rock 'n' rollers.

The Hells Angels being employed as security: In retrospect this decision was probably not wise.

QUOTABLES

"Who's fighting and what for?"

Mick Jagger to the crowd at the Altamont concert, after several fights had broken out in front of the stage.

TOP MOVIE COUPLES

Even if you haven't seen the film, you probably know these famous couples.

♥ **Vivien Leigh and Clark Gable (as Scarlett O'Hara and Rhett Butler),** *Gone With the Wind* She's a feisty and independent Southern plantation owner, he's a cocky and determined businessman. The combination is hot. (See page 14.)

♥ **Dustin Hoffman and Anne Bancroft (as Benjamin Braddock and Mrs. Robinson),** *The Graduate* A recent college grad is seduced by a sexy, married friend of the family. (See page 55.)

♥ **Billy Crystal and Meg Ryan (as Harry Burns and Sally Albright),** *When Harry Met Sally...* The wise-cracking Harry and the uptight Sally hate each other when they first meet, but after many years of friendship realize they belong together.

♥ **Bud Cort and Ruth Gordon (as Harold and Maude),** *Harold and Maude* A death-obsessed twentysomething oddball meets a life-loving eccentric in her late seventies. (See page 84.)

♥ **Humphrey Bogart and Ingrid Bergman (as Rick Blaine and Ilsa Lund),** *Casablanca* A cynical American bar owner in Casablanca and the beautiful wife of a leader of the World War II fascist resistance movement are former lovers reunited only to realize, painfully, that they can't be together. (See page 20.)

♥ **Glenn Close and Michael Douglas (as Alex Forrest and Dan Gallager),** *Fatal Attraction* A hot extramarital encounter between professional colleagues devolves into a bunny being boiled. Consider it the ultimate "that was a big mistake" affair.

♥ **Ryan O'Neal and Ali MacGraw (as Oliver Barrett IV and Jennifer Cavalleri),** *Love Story* Two Harvard and Radcliffe students fall in love, get married, and have tragedy strike when one of them gets cancer—and dies.

♥ **Warren Beatty and Faye Dunaway (as Bonnie and Clyde),** *Bonnie and Clyde* Two sexy, Depression-era bank robbers go on a killing spree across the country. (See page 58.)

♥ William Powell and Myrna Loy (as Nick and Nora Charles), The Thin Man movies
This stylish pair in a series of 1930s screwball mystery movies cracked jokes, solved crimes, and always had time for a martini. Their trusty dog Asta was never far behind.

♥ Robert Redford and Barbra Streisand (as Hubbell Gardner and Katie Morosky), *The Way We Were*
The dashing military guy/writer Hubbel and smart, headstrong political activist Katie are drawn together despite their differences, then marry and have a child. But even though they will probably always love each other, they realize they aren't meant to be.

♥ Katharine Hepburn and Cary Grant (as various characters), *The Philadelphia Story* and *Bringing Up Baby*
She's beautiful and spunky, he's suave and handsome—which means they're great to watch. (See more about *Bringing Up Baby* on page 8.)

♥ Woody Allen and Diane Keaton (as Alvy Singer and Annie Hall), *Annie Hall*
Two crazy, quirky urbanites fall in and out of love in 1970s New York City. (See page 115.)

Clark Gable and Vivien Leigh as Rhett Butler and Scarlett O'Hara in *Gone With the Wind*.

WHAT IT'S ABOUT

The setting is a futuristic England, and Alex and his gang (the droogs) are serious menaces to society. They like to hang out at the Korova Milk Bar, sip amphetamine-laced dairy cocktails, and then engage in what Alex refers to as "a bit of the old ultra-violence," which ranges from property destruction to senseless beatings and rape. Alex is eventually sent to prison, where he volunteers for an experimental government-sponsored rehabilitation treatment, which involves restraining him, forcing his eyes open with metal clamps, and showing him violent and sexual films. The idea is to reprogram him to be repulsed by these things and release him back into society, reformed. Unfortunately, one of Alex's only loves, Beethoven's 9th Symphony, is played during one of his treatment sessions, and as a result he ends up being repulsed by that as well.

The reprogramming seems to work, but when Alex is let out, he is not equipped for the violent world he left behind. When one of Alex's past victims learns he is tortured by the 9th Symphony, he forces Alex to listen to it, and Alex attempts suicide. At the hospital, he is visited by a government official who, facing public criticism, apologizes to Alex, and promises him a good life if he helps fix the government's image. As a gift, the official plays the 9th Symphony for Alex, who then has a weird sexual fantasy: His old nature has returned.

A Clockwork Orange is based on Anthony Burgess' 1962 novel of the same name.

Who's In It

Malcolm McDowell as Alex De Large

Patrick Magee as Mr. Alexander

Michael Bates as Chief Guard

Warren Clarke as Dim

Adrienne Corri as Mrs. Alexander

Carl Duering as Dr. Brodsky

Miriam Karlin as Catlady

More Directed by Stanley Kubrick

Dr. Strangelove or *How I Learned to Stop Worrying and Love the Bomb* (1964)
2001: A Space Odyssey (1968, page 67)
The Shining (1980, page 135)
Full Metal Jacket (1987)

WHY ALL THE FUSS?

- It is a really sinister mix of violent realism and bizarre sci-fi futuristic fable.

- Stanley Kubrick's surprising use of uplifting music by Beethoven and other classical artists made the droogs' amoral behavior all the more horrifying.

- The movie addresses free will and the question of whose right it is to reprogram whom.

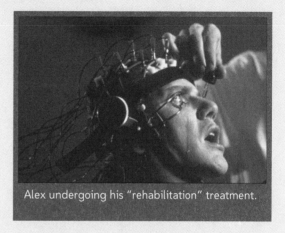
Alex undergoing his "rehabilitation" treatment.

- It also offers a critique of modern and behavioral psychology, showing a world in which the government enlists science to control members of society, modify their behavior, and remove their individuality. (Alex is a monster who expresses his free will by doing despicable things, but does the government have the right to erase his personality?)

- Additionally, it questions whether modern psychology is actually effective in altering a person's behavior. (Afterall, Alex is not really cured in the end.)

- It got critical attention. The film was nominated somewhat controversially (due to its graphic sexual and violent content) for four Academy Awards: Best Picture, Best Director, Best Adapted Screenplay, and Best Editing.

- Kubrick got a lot of heat for what many saw as the film's glamorization of violence; others saw the movie as a satirical, critical take on an increasingly violent society and people's insensitivity to it. Kubrick didn't say much about it, but when copycat crimes happened in England, he withdrew the movie from the country, and it became illegal to show *A Clockwork Orange* in the UK for more than two decades. (The ban has since been lifted.)

THE STUFF PEOPLE STILL TALK ABOUT

The clothes of the droogs: Scary all-white outfits with codpieces, suspenders, and black bowler hats. The costumes are now iconic and are all over the place on Halloween. Even Bart Simpson has donned a droog get-up.

The murder scene: Alex brutally kills a woman using a large white statue of a penis. Once you've seen it, it's kind of hard to forget.

Alex's rehabilitation: His eyes are held open by metal clamps (and kept wet with drops) as he's shown violent, disturbing images.

Alex's love for the music of Beethoven: Despite being such a disgusting thug, Alex also has a passion for this beautiful music, until his treatment turns him against it.

★ Barbra Streisand was among the celebs who refused to present the Oscar for Best Picture, citing the fact that this horribly offensive movie was one of the nominees.

★ *The French Connection* won Best Picture and Best Director that year. In his acceptance speech, the film's director, William Friedkin, praised Kubrick as the best director of the year, and, basically, the best director—period.

★ Bands who have borrowed the look of the droogs include Gnarls Barkley, My Chemical Romance, and Blur.

QUOTABLES

*"Goodness comes from within.
When a man cannot choose, he ceases to be a man."*
The prison chaplain tells Alex this when discussing the experimental treatment.

"I was cured all right."
Alex says this in the final moment of the movie, when he realizes—after having a graphic sex fantasy—that his deprogramming didn't work. He's "cured" from his cure.

1971

WILLY WONKA AND THE CHOCOLATE FACTORY

DIRECTOR: MEL STUART

SCREENWRITER: ROALD DAHL

WHAT IT'S ABOUT

World-famous, eccentric candy maker Willy Wonka launches a contest awarding its winners a tour of his amazing chocolate factory—and a lifetime supply of chocolate. Five winning tickets are hidden in Wonka chocolate bars around the world, and thousands of kids everywhere are vying for them. Among the winners are gluttonous Augustus Gloop, TV-obsessed Mike Teevee, bratty Veruca Salt, spoiled Violet Beauregarde, and a poor kid named Charlie Bucket. The kids, along with their parental escorts (Charlie brings his grandfather) are taken inside the factory by Wonka, a total weirdo who speaks in riddles and wears a top hat and a purple coat.

Inside the factory, the kids witness a candy world beyond their wildest dreams with a giant flowing chocolate river, Technicolor candy vegetation, and gummy bear trees. But when the children behave badly, they are punished in rather gruesome ways, like being shrunken, inflated, and sucked into the chocolate river. At the end of the tour, only Charlie remains, but even he must prove to Wonka that he is worthy of Wonka's true prize of the contest. After Charlie passes one final test, Wonka explains that the whole contest and the day's events were his way of finding a child trustworthy enough to take over the factory for him.

Willy Wonka and the Chocolate Factory is based on Dahl's novel *Charlie and the Chocolate Factory*.

Who's In It

Gene Wilder as
Willy Wonka

Jack Albertson as
Grandpa Joe

Peter Ostrum as
Charlie Bucket

Julie Dawn Cole as
Veruca Salt

Paris Themmen as
Mike Teevee

Michael Bollner as
Augustus Gloop

Denise Nickerson as
Violet Beauregarde

More With Gene Wilder

Bonnie and Clyde (1967, page 58)
The Producers (1968)
Blazing Saddles (1974)
Young Frankenstein (1974)
Stir Crazy (1980)

WHY ALL THE FUSS?

It is one of the greatest children's movies ever made, including awesome visuals of a colorful candy haven, disturbing (and yet rewarding) scenes of bad kids being punished for being jerks, great characters such as the orange little men who work for Wonka, and a classic story of goodness being triumphant.

Wilder as Wonka is brilliantly creepy. He talks in riddles, seems to enjoy when bad kids get what's coming to them, and obviously doesn't mind if his guests are scared out of their minds every once in a while.

Besides being a children's flick, the movie had mass adult appeal, as it was filled with sophisticated, sharp-tongued humor.

The songs—like "Pure Imagination" and "Oompa Loompa Doompa Dee Do"— have gone down in history and helped score an Oscar nomination.

Bonus Material

★ The movie was financed by Quaker Oats as a vehicle to introduce a new chocolate bar, which the company never produced. (Nestlé later bought the rights and now produces Wonka-branded candy.)

★ The first actor considered for the role of Willy Wonka was Joel Grey, who played the Master of Ceremonies in *Cabaret*, but it was decided that he wasn't physically imposing enough to play the candy man.

★ The chocolate river in the movie was a mixture of chocolate ice cream, 150,000 buckets of water, and an anti-bubble formula.

THE STUFF PEOPLE STILL TALK ABOUT

The Oompa Loompas: Wonka's bizarre band of miniature helpers who have orange skin and green hair.

The Violet scene: Violet Beauregarde eats a piece of candy she shouldn't have and becomes very inflated and very blue.

Mike Teevee: A kid who is shrunk down to the size of a candy bar, after insisting on being transmitted across a room via TV waves.

Veruca Salt: The bratty, demanding girl who was the inspiration for the name of the American 1990s indie rock band.

The boat ride: Wonka takes his guests on a scary and psychedelic trip through a dark tunnel on the chocolate river, and sings about the fires of hell and the grim reaper.

Willy Wonka and his beloved Oompa Loompas.

QUOTABLES

"I said, 'Good day!'"

This is Wonka's way of saying "Good-bye and get out" to Charlie's grandfather, Grandpa Joe, after Grandpa questions Wonka about why Charlie did not get his prize.

"The snozberries taste like snozberries!"

Willy Wonka says this when telling his guests about the lickable wallpaper lining the hallway, which is made of a fruit called snozberries.

"We are the music makers, and we are the dreamers of dreams."

Willy Wonka says this to Veruca Salt after she has ridiculed the idea of a fruit called a "snozberry."

1971

HAROLD AND MAUDE

DIRECTOR: HAL ASHBY

SCREENWRITER: COLIN HIGGINS

WHAT IT'S ABOUT

Harold is a rich, depressed early twentysomething obsessed with death. He continually and comically stages fake suicide attempts, which are barely acknowledged by his annoyed mother. Naturally, he likes to attend the funerals of people he doesn't know, and, while doing so, he meets kindred spirit 79-year-old Maude, who also goes to funerals just for kicks. The feisty Maude teaches Harold—through stealing cars, saving trees, and more—how to live and savor life. The two form an unconventional friendship and, ultimately, a love affair. The ending is sad and beautiful, as Harold becomes forced to live without Maude when at 80 she decides it is time to die and poisons herself. Harold is left to embrace life on his own, which it now seems he may be able to do thanks to Maude.

Who's In It

Ruth Gordon as
Maude

Bud Cort as
Harold Chasen

Vivian Pickles as
Mrs. Chasen

Cyril Cusak as
Glaucus

Charles Tyner as
Uncle Victor

More Directed by Hal Ashby

The Last Detail (1973)
Shampoo (1975)
Coming Home (1978)
Being There (1979)

More With Ruth Gordon

Rosemary's Baby (1968)
Every Which Way But Loose (1978)

★ The movie bombed when it came out. Movie industry magazine *Variety* wrote, "It has all the fun and gaiety of a burning orphanage." When college kids took an interest in it many years later, it resurfaced as a cult masterpiece.

WHY ALL THE FUSS?

Harold and Maude is perhaps best known for its strange love story between a rebellious old lady and a repressed young guy and the fact that they are actually getting it on. The cinematic love affair is also considered one of the greatest of all time.

The movie also became a cult classic for its dark, deadpan humor. It features a main character staging his own (fake) death via hanging, as well as pretending to set himself on fire, slit his wrists, perform hari-kari, and chop off his hand to get some kind of reaction out of his rich, preoccupied mother. Sometimes, he does these things in front of guests and blind dates his mother has selected. Also, he drives a hearse.

One theater in Minneapolis played the film for three years straight.

This movie paved the way for later deadpan, dark-humored films with quirky characters like *Rushmore*, *The Royal Tenenbaums*, and *Little Miss Sunshine*.

Bonus Material

★ Writer Colin Higgins went on to direct '80s movies *Foul Play* and *9 to 5*.

★ Higgins originally wrote the basis for the movie as a master's thesis at UCLA when he was 28.

★ It's Mary's favorite movie in the film *There's Something About Mary*.

Harold and Maude meet for the first time—at a random stranger's funeral.

THE STUFF PEOPLE STILL TALK ABOUT

The opening credits: The audience is introduced to Harold by watching him prepare for and attempt his suicide by hanging. It is only until his mother comes in, sees him, and basically ignores him, that it's clear an actual suicide has not occurred—and that Harold is a really odd dude.

Cat Stevens' soundtrack: Now known as Yusuf Islam, Stevens contributed songs to the movie's soundtrack that are now forever linked to it, most notably, "If You Want to Sing Out, Sing Out."

The performances: Ruth Gordon and Bud Cort were both brilliant as totally eccentric weirdos.

QUOTABLES

"I suppose you think that's very funny, Harold."

Harold's mother says this casually when she walks in and sees him fake hanging himself at the beginning of the movie.

"A lot of people enjoy being dead. But they are not dead, really. They're just backing away from life. Reach out. Take a chance. Get hurt even. But play as well as you can. Go, team, go! Give me an 'L'! Give me an 'I'! Give me a 'V'! Give me an 'E'! L-I-V-E. LIVE! Otherwise, you got nothing to talk about in the locker room."

Maude says this to Harold. It's one of the many times she tries to communicate her life philosophy to him.

WHAT IT'S ABOUT

In this sweeping epic, Michael Corleone, the son of big mafia don Vito Corleone, has just returned from World War II to New York City and is ready to get on with civilian life. He's never been a part of the "family business"—i.e., the mafia—and he wants to keep it that way. But when Vito is shot and wounded for refusing to be a part of a drug-trafficking operation, Michael goes after the men who tried to murder his dad, and he kills them. Michael then escapes to Sicily to hide.

Back in New York, the killings have set off bloody mob wars, and the eldest Corleone son, Sonny, is brutally killed. Vito calls a summit of all the mafia families demanding a truce—in large part because he wants Michael to be safe when he returns from Italy—and a peace is achieved. When Michael returns, he takes over the responsibilities of his ailing father and is determined to legitimize the business by running casinos and hotels in Las Vegas. But soon Michael's life is in danger, so he decides to "settle all family business" by having each and every rival killed. With this act, he fully assumes the role he never wanted—don of the Corleone family in New York.

The Godfather is based on Mario Puzo's 1969 novel of the same name. (Puzo also cowrote the screenplay for Superman, page 121.)

Who's In It

Marlon Brando as
Don Vito Corleone

Al Pacino as
Michael Corleone

Robert Duvall as
Tom Hagen

Richard Castellano as
Peter Clemenza

James Caan as
Sonny Corleone

Diane Keaton as
Kay Adams

Richard Conte as
Don Emilio Barzini

More Directed by Francis Ford Coppola

The Conversation (1974)
The Godfather: Part II (1974)
Apocalypse Now (1979)
The Outsiders (1983)
Rumble Fish (1983)

WHY ALL THE FUSS?

The Godfather changed the way people looked at the mafia forever, taking audiences inside the workings of organized crime, and glamorizing it, for the first time. Every mafia movie or TV show since—*GoodFellas, Scarface, Carlito's Way, The Sopranos, The Departed*, and even comedies like *My Cousin Vinny* and *Analyze This*—has been influenced by this film.

It contains some of the most famous scenes and quoted lines in movie history, which have been referenced and parodied everywhere, including in shows like *The Simpsons, South Park*, and *Seinfeld*, and in commercials for products such as Audi cars and Pepsi.

The film featured Al Pacino, Robert Duvall, James Caan, and Marlon Brando, who were all nominated for Academy Awards. In fact, the movie was nominated for a whopping 11 Academy Awards altogether. It won three: Best Picture, Best Screenplay, and Best Actor (Marlon Brando).

Bonus Material

★ The baby baptized at the end of the movie is the director's daughter, Sofia Coppola—now a director herself of films such as *Lost in Translation* and *The Virgin Suicides*.

★ Studio executives wanted to cast either Burt Lancaster, Orson Welles, or George C. Scott as Vito Corleone, but Coppola insisted on Laurence Olivier or Marlon Brando.

★ The cat that Vito is petting during the opening of the movie was not part of the script; Brando found the stray on set, and it became part of the scene.

★ Michael Corleone's girlfriend/wife is played by Diane Keaton, who plays a very different role in the movie *Annie Hall* (page 115). It's hard to believe she's the same person.

THE STUFF PEOPLE STILL TALK ABOUT

The murder montage: At the end of the movie, Coppola cuts between Michael Corleone participating in the baptism of his nephew and several brutal revenge killings of Michael's adversaries. The combination emphasizes the gore of the killings, as well as Michael's new power and his ability to wear two faces (he ordered the hits but is calmly participating in a service at a church and renouncing Satan to a priest).

The horse head scene: The movie executive who won't give Vito's friend a role in a film wakes up with the bloody head of his prized horse in his bed. (The friend gets the part.)

Brando's performance: He spoke in a signature raspy voice, his cheeks filled with specially designed dental implants that puffed out his mouth and made him sound weird.

Sonny's death: Mafia member Sonny is brutally slain at a tollbooth in a bloody, unexpected mob hit.

The movie's operatic music: The calm, serious violin-filled music still instantly invokes the feeling of the epic, multi-generational movie.

Don Vito Corleone accepting a cordial greeting.

QUOTABLES

"I'm gonna make him an offer he can't refuse."

Vito Corleone says this about a movie executive who won't give his friend a role in a film.
(The "offer"—a terrifying threat—does, in fact, change the exec's mind.)
Later, Michael uses this same line.

"It's not personal, Sonny, it's strictly business."

Michael tells Sonny this before the killing of a crooked cop and a druglord.
This line is repeated throughout the film and has become a part of the
lingo in mafia-themed movies.

"Leave the gun, take the cannoli."

After two mobsters carry out a hit in a car, one says this to the other. It shows how routine
committing murder is to these guys.

Sonny: "What the hell is this?"
Tessio: "It's a Sicilian message.
It means Luca Brasi sleeps with the fishes."

This exchange takes place when the Corleones receive a dead fish wrapped in the bullet-proof
vest of Luca Brasi, a member of the Corleone crew. It means that Brasi has been killed, as
the mob often disposed of dead bodies in the water.

★ To make a political statement, Brando famously refused to accept his Oscar and sent an
Apache activist named Satcheen Littlefeather to reject it as a protest to the film industry's
mistreatment of Native Americans, a cause he was rallying around at the time. Thing is, she
wasn't Native American, she was a B-movie actress who would later appear in *Playboy*.

THE EXORCIST
DIRECTOR: WILLIAM FRIEDKIN
SCREENWRITER: WILLIAM PETER BLATTY

WHAT IT'S ABOUT

Chris MacNeil, a successful actress, is living with daughter Regan in the Washington, DC, neighborhood of Georgetown while shooting a movie. Regan suddenly starts exhibiting strange behavior: peeing on the carpet in front of dinner guests, levitating in bed, and muscling up superhuman strength. Then, she just happens to be present while her babysitter is killed.

Chris takes Regan for tests at a hospital, and psychiatrists are brought in, but things only get worse. Desperate for help, Chris approaches a local Catholic priest named Father Karras about the idea of an exorcism, the process of casting out a demon that has inhabited a human being. Karras is hesitant at first but agrees to see Regan and encounters a thing that looks nothing like a young girl, speaks in a weird gravelly voice, vomits all over him, and claims to be the devil. Eventually, an exorcism is scheduled with Karras and an experienced senior priest named Father Merrin. The two men do spiritual battle with Regan—who at this point is a foul-mouthed, deformed, violent creature who can do things like spin her head around and float through the air. The movie ends with Regan being saved from whatever demon possessed her but not without cost: Karras sacrifices himself by letting the demon enter his body and jumping out a window to his death.

Who's In It

Ellen Burstyn as
Chris MacNeil

Linda Blair as
Regan Teresa MacNeil

Jason Miller as
Father Karras

Max von Sydow as
Father Merrin

More With
Ellen Burstyn

The Last Picture Show (1971)
*Alice Doesn't Live Here
Anymore* (1974)
*Requiem for
a Dream* (2000)

The Exorcist is based on Blatty's novel of the same name.

WHY ALL THE FUSS?

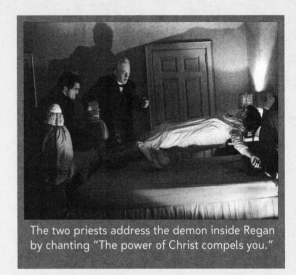

The two priests address the demon inside Regan by chanting "The power of Christ compels you."

- The movie was so shocking that it literally had audience members shrieking, passing out, and vomiting in the aisles. (And then they'd come back and see it again.)

- *The Exorcist* introduced the now-familiar theme of the evil child (Damien, the kid in the Omen series is just one later example of this).

- Now considered one of the most frightening movies of all time, *The Exorcist* was also a phenomenon when it was released and became the first major blockbuster in horror-movie history.

- The film was a critical success; it won Oscars for Best Screenplay and Best Sound, and was nominated for eight others, including Best Picture, Best Director, Best Actress, Best Supporting Actor, and Best Supporting Actress.

THE STUFF PEOPLE STILL TALK ABOUT

Regan's most revolting moments: Turning her head a complete 360 degrees; vomiting green ooze; masturbating with a crucifix; floating above the bed; unleashing countless foul obscenities.

The movie's distinct and chilling score: It features the sound of a solo piano, which is the opening phrase of a composition by musician Mike Oldfield called "Tubular Bells." After being incorporated into the film's soundtrack, it became known as the "Theme From the Exorcist."

The exorcism scene: Father Merrin and Damien Karras have a final showdown with Regan that includes Regan levitating, someone being killed, and lots of cursing.

★ Director William Friedkin attempted to alter young actress Linda Blair's voice to get the voice of the demon, but it didn't work. He called in actress Mercedes McCambridge, who worked in a sound booth for three weeks chain-smoking, swallowing raw eggs, and being tied to a chair to produce the voice heard in the film.

★ Many of the sound effects used in the film were created with simple and unconventional "instruments"; the sound of Regan's head turning around is an old wallet full of credit cards being twisted.

QUOTABLES

"The power of Christ compels you!"

Fathers Merrin and Karras say this line and variations on it when they are attempting to defeat the demon possessing Regan. It's the type of line people say when walking out of the movie theater.

1975

JAWS

DIRECTOR: STEVEN SPIELBERG

SCREENWRITER: CARL GOTTLIER

WHAT IT'S ABOUT

The July Fourth weekend is approaching and vacation destination Amity Island has a bit of a problem—just before the weekend, a local girl gets devoured by a shark. The police chief, Martin Brody, wants to close the beaches until the problem is under control, but the town's mayor refuses, thinking of all the tourist money that could be lost. However, the number of people likely being claimed by shark attacks keeps rising—a young boy, a fisherman, and a boater all meet gruesome and untimely deaths. A crusty bounty hunter named Quint (who survived a shark attack that took the lives of hundreds of men when his boat went down in WWII) and oceanographer Matt Hooper (a rich kid who has a fascination with sharks) are brought in to help Brody, who happens to be afraid of the ocean, take the shark down.

The trio sets out in a leaky vessel and meets Jaws face to face. The men attempt to poison the Great White with a dart but fail, and the boat becomes badly damaged by the shark. Soon, they are going under. Hooper escapes Jaws by hiding underwater, while Quint is consumed by the great white. Finally, Brody ingeniously lodges an air tank in Jaws' mouth and explodes it with a well-aimed shot—shark bits fly, and Brody and Hooper make their way back to shore.

Who's In It

Roy Scheider as Martin Brody

Richard Dreyfuss as Matt Hooper

Robert Shaw as Quint

Murray Hamilton as Mayor Vaughn

More Directed by Steven Spielberg

Close Encounters of the Third Kind (1977)
Raiders of the Lost Ark (1981, page 130)
E.T.: The Extra-Terrestrial (1982)
Jurassic Park (1993)
Saving Private Ryan (1998)

Jaws is based on Peter Benchely's 1974 novel of the same name.

WHY ALL THE FUSS?

It was scary. People were afraid to go swimming in the ocean for years. And then the sequel came out.

The filmmaking was innovative. Viewers rarely see the shark, and Spielberg's ability to make the shark scary without showing it has been considered brilliant. Additionally, when audiences did finally see the shark (which was actually a mechanical model), the big fish was quite convincing.

Jaws was the first summer blockbuster. Thanks to advance advertising on television networks and the decision to open the movie on more than 400 screens at once, it became the largest-grossing film to date when it was released. After this, every big studio started using these types of promotional tactics to gain audiences for new films.

Jaws won a lot of acclaim. It was nominated for Best Picture, and won Oscars for Best Editing, Best Score, and Best Sound.

Bonus Material

★ The shark was portrayed by three different mechanical, rubber models, all of which were dubbed "Bruce."

★ The tale Quint tells about the USS *Indianapolis* (see next page) is based on a historical event, but the date is incorrect; in the movie, he says it happened on June 29, 1945, but it actually took place a month later on July 30.

★ Director Steven Spielberg was only 27 years old when he directed the film. He had made a couple of movies before *Jaws*, but this was the film that put him on the map.

THE STUFF PEOPLE STILL TALK ABOUT

John Williams' haunting, droning score: The *Jaws* theme (da-da...da-da...da-da...da-da) is now instantly recognizable and synonymous with the idea of something dangerous lurking out of sight. The movie *Airplane!* spoofs the music and the movie in its opening shots: a plane's wing slices through a cloudy sky, referencing a shark's fin moving through the water.

Quint's speech: Out at sea with Hooper and Brody, Quint recalls the horrifying tale of when his WWII ship, the USS *Indianapolis*, was shot down by the Japanese right after it had delivered the atom bomb, and hundreds of men were eaten alive by sharks.

Brody hangs on for his life as Jaws goes in for the kill.

QUOTABLES

"You're gonna need a bigger boat."

Brody says this to Quint, after seeing how big the shark really is. At this point, it's too late to get a bigger boat.

"Smile, you son of a [bang]!"

Brody yells at Jaws, firing his gun and hoping to hit the oxygen tank the shark has in its mouth, in his one last chance at defeating the shark.

ROCKY HORROR PICTURE SHOW
DIRECTOR: JIM SHARMAN
SCREENWRITERS: JIM SHARMAN AND RICHARD O'BRIEN

WHAT IT'S ABOUT

Newly engaged Brad Majors and Janet Weiss are on a road trip when their car breaks down on a country road in Denton, Ohio. Soon they are stuck in a storm. They seek a phone and shelter in a nearby castle, home to transvestite mad scientist Dr. Frank-N-Furter, who just happens to be hosting a Transylvanian convention, a gathering of people from Transylvania. (Transylvania is an area in Romania that's known for being home to the fictional character Dracula.) The convention guests are all in costumes of some sort and wearing goth makeup, black formal wear, and fishnet stockings. Frank greets the couple in a musical number, singing, "I'm just a sweet transvestite from transsexual Transylvania."

Janet and Brad are plunged into the wild and wacky world of Frank and his underlings. In between and during raunchy, glam-rock musical numbers, Frank strips the couple to their underwear, shows them "Rocky" (a buff blond guy Frank created for his own pleasure), seduces both of them, and serves them a dinner of a guy he killed earlier—a science experiment gone wrong. Along the way, the innocent Janet is awakened sexually, and she hooks up with Rocky. The night takes an even darker (and weirder) turn when Frank's underlings Riff-Raff and Magenta revolt, revealing their true identities: They're actually aliens from the *planet* Transsexual in the galaxy of Transylvania, not from the earthly Transylvania. Then, the freaky pair kills the doctor and magically blasts off in the castle to fly back home. Brad and Janet watch from the ground.

Who's In It

Tim Curry as
Dr. Frank-N-Furter

Susan Sarandon as
Janet Weiss

Barry Bostwick as
Brad Majors

Richard O'Brien as
Riff-Raff

Patricia Quinn as
Magenta

Nell Campbell as
Columbia

Peter Hinwood as
Rocky

More With
Susan Sarandon

Bull Durham (1988)
White Palace (1990)
Thelma & Louise (1991)
Dead Man Walking (1995)
Enchanted (2007)

WHY ALL THE FUSS?

Truthfully, *Rocky Horror* (as it's often called) is not really that great of a movie. It's the *Rocky Horror* phenomenon that cemented the movie in pop culture history. While it bombed big time when it came out, it was later re-released as a midnight movie and at the height of its popularity was screened in 250 theaters across the country. Crowds all around the world still line up to see it.

It has some really bizarre, fun musical numbers, in which the convention guests demonstrate the "Time Warp" dance, Janet and Rocky get it on, and Frank dances around in makeup, pearls, black bikini briefs, and a mesh corsetlike item.

Tim Curry's performance as Frank is wild and weird (as is pretty much the whole movie).

Rocky Horror spawned the interactive movie experience. Showings became events, with audience members dressing up as the film's characters, acting out the movie as it played, talking back to the screen, and throwing items such as rice, toilet paper, and toast at the screen during key points in the movie. Other movies now screened as sing-a-longs include *The Sound of Music*, *The Wizard of Oz*, *West Side Story*, and *Grease*.

QUOTABLES

"Dammit, Janet."

Brad says this to Janet in the opening musical number in which he proposes to her.

"I'm just a sweet transvestite from transsexual Transylvania."

Frank sings this to Brad and Janet, in his grand, introductory musical number.
It's not your everyday introduction.

THE STUFF PEOPLE STILL TALK ABOUT

The movie's cult status: People saw the movie hundreds of times, and theaters played it for years on end—in some cases, as long as two decades straight.

The movie's signature songs: "Time Warp," "Sweet Transvestite," and "Touch-a Touch-a Touch Me" are not your standard musical numbers.

The narrator: An older man occasionally interrupts the action to further explain the evening's events. (He also helps demonstrate the "Time Warp.")

Dr. Frank-N-Furter welcomes the innocent Brad and Janet to his underworld.

Susan Sarandon as Janet: Long, long before she became the huge movie star and political activist she is today, she appeared in this film.

★ People who are attending the *Rocky Horror* experience at a theater for the first time are referred to as "virgins" and are sometimes subjected to initiation rituals, like getting a "V" written on their forehead or being made to suck the cream out of a Twinkie.

★ A low-level marketing executive at production company 20th Century Fox came up with the highly successful idea to show *Rocky Horror* (which had been a total flop) as a midnight movie.

★ The Clinton Street Theater in Portland, Oregon, has screened *Rocky Horror* every Saturday night since 1978.

MONTY PYTHON AND THE HOLY GRAIL

DIRECTORS: TERRY GILLIAM AND TERRY JONES

SCREENWRITERS: GRAHAM CHAPMAN, JOHN CLEESE, ERIC IDLE, TERRY GILLIAM, TERRY JONES, AND MICHAEL PALIN

WHAT IT'S ABOUT

King Arthur, the mythical British leader of medieval England, travels the land searching for the finest men to serve in his posse, known as the Knights of the Round Table. Along the way, he meets a variety of ridiculous characters, including one called the Black Knight, a knight who will just not die, and castle guards who know way too much about the flight patterns of swallows. After Arthur has finally assembled his crew of knights, God appears to the group and tells Arthur that he must find the Holy Grail, a religious artifact.

The group searches for it unsuccessfully and then splits up, each member having his own absurd adventure while doing so. The men do battle with a killer bunny, use a Holy Hand Grenade, face a deadly pop quiz, and arrive at a castle guarded by some insult-hurling French soldiers met earlier in the film. There are also fart jokes, musical numbers about Camelot, and lots of references to the fact that the movie is a movie. The film abruptly ends when some modern-day British police enter the climactic battle scene and arrest the men for the death of a medieval historian (who appeared earlier in the film to provide commentary on King Arthur and was violently killed by the knights).

Who's In It

John Cleese as Sir Lancelot and others

Eric Idle as Sir Robin and others

Graham Chapman as King Arthur and others

Terry Jones as Sir Bedevere and others

Terry Gilliam as the Green Knight and others

Michael Palin as Sir Galahad and others

More From Monty Python

Monty Python's Flying Circus (1969-1974)
Life of Brian (1979)
The Meaning of Life (1983)

WHY ALL THE FUSS?

Monty Python was already a famous humor group with an absurdist TV sketch comedy show in England called *Monty Python's Flying Circus* when the group made this movie. This movie was just as nonsensical, ridiculous, and smart as the show, and it became a cult classic.

The movie includes iconic comic characters such as The Knights Who Say "Ni" (who are tortured when they hear the word "it"); the ferocious killer bunny; and the determined Black Knight who, even after his arms and legs have been cut off, wishes to keep fighting.

This brand of intentionally absurd self-referential humor influenced everything from comedy troupes like *Kids in the Hall* and *The State* to the skits on *Saturday Night Live* and *MADtv*. It has also been referenced in many movies, including *Shrek 3* and *Harold and Kumar Escape From Guantanamo Bay*. (There's also a lot of quoting from this movie that happens on college campuses.)

Bonus Material

★ In the movie, King Arthur does not have a horse; instead, he walks with a servant trailing behind, clicking two coconuts together to make the "clip-clop" sound of a horse's hooves. Though the gag was funny, the decision to use the coconuts was made because the movie had no money for real horses.

★ A 2004 fan survey conducted by Amazon UK and the Internet Movie Database named the movie the best British film of all time.

The group on its quest for the Holy Grail.

THE STUFF PEOPLE STILL TALK ABOUT

The bunny scene: A cute, innocent-looking rabbit attacks the men, demonstrating that it is—as they were warned—a ferocious killer bunny.

The silly animations: Monty Python member Terry Gilliam created absurd cartoons that appear throughout the film (often between the knights' different adventures), and these became a hallmark of Monty Python's work.

The script: To this day, people still recite random lines and entire scenes from this movie.

QUOTABLES

"It's just a flesh wound."

The Black Knight says this to Arthur, who has just cut off both of the Knight's arms.
Clearly, it is more than a flesh wound.

"I fart in your general direction. Your mother was a hamster and your father smelt of elderberries."

A French soldier says this to King Arthur to try to dissuade Arthur from entering the soldier's castle.
This makes no sense and is not at all threatening.

"We are the Knights who say 'Ni!'"

The leader of the Knights of Ni says this when King Arthur comes upon them in the woods,
and it appears that every time he says "Ni" it causes pain to King Arthur's crew.
So, he says it repeatedly. Again, makes no sense.

1976 TAXI DRIVER
DIRECTOR: MARTIN SCORSESE

SCREENWRITER: PAUL SCHRADER

WHAT IT'S ABOUT

Travis Bickle, a 26-year-old ex-Marine who just served in Vietnam, is a depressed and unstable loner who lives in New York City and frequents the local pornographic movie theater. He takes a job driving a cab at night to deal with his insomnia but gets increasingly disgusted by the pimps, hookers, drug addicts, and robbers he sees nightly on the streets.

In his desperate state of loneliness, he attempts to court a presidential candidate's aide but screws it up by taking her to a porno on their first date (smooth!). He later becomes fixated on Iris, an underage prostitute whom he tries to talk into quitting the business. Travis becomes increasingly isolated from the world and trapped in his own mind, which becomes apparent through voice-overs that reveal his own internal monologue of anguish and hate. In a plan to rebel against the dark forces that surround him, he starts working out and buys a bunch of guns, as well as shaves his head into a mohawk. He slowly slips into full-blown madness, attempting to kill the presidential candidate whose aide he was dating and going on a massive shooting spree in an effort to save Iris from the world of prostitution. Despite his madness, he manages to become a lauded hero in the newspapers.

Who's In It

Robert De Niro as Travis Bickle

Jodie Foster as Iris

Harvey Keitel as Sport

Cybill Shepherd as Betsy

Albert Brooks as Tom

More With Robert De Niro

Mean Streets (1973)
The Godfather: Part II (1974)
Raging Bull (1980)
The King of Comedy (1982)
GoodFellas (1990, page 159)
A Bronx Tale (1993)

More With Jodie Foster

Freaky Friday (1976)
The Accused (1988)
The Silence of the Lambs (1991, page 163)
Panic Room (2002)
Inside Man (2006)

WHY ALL THE FUSS?

Travis is one of the most alienated, lonely, and disturbed characters ever captured on film. Yet, he's also relatable, which makes his character all that more unsettling.

Martin Scorsese used cool cinematic techniques. He subtly brought audiences inside Travis' head using voice-over, shots from the character's point of view, and techniques such as slow motion and tight close-ups. The result is creepy and claustrophobic.

The movie had a great cast, including a young Robert De Niro in one of his first major roles, and a 12-year-old Jodie Foster, who famously played the young prostitute.

The movie was nominated for four Oscars: Best Picture, Best Actor (De Niro), Best Supporting Actress (Foster), and Best Music.

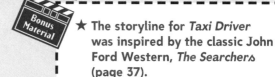

★ The storyline for *Taxi Driver* was inspired by the classic John Ford Western, *The Searchers* (page 37).

★ Director Scorsese plays a passenger in Travis' cab who has Travis stop at a building to watch the passenger's wife through her lover's apartment window from the back of the cab.

★ De Niro improvised the famous "You talkin' to me?" monologue.

★ Foster's role inspired John Hinkley Jr. to shoot former president Ronald Reagan. The delusional Hinkley hoped that shooting the president would win the attention and admiration of Foster, with whom he was obsessed.

THE STUFF PEOPLE STILL TALK ABOUT

The NYC driving sequences: Travis takes his cab all around New York late at night, observing all the "scum" of society, i.e., the drug dealers, drug users, and pimps.

Travis' mohawk: We first see his new hairdo at a presidential rally. At first, he is shown only from the neck down. When the camera pans up, he is sporting a fresh mohawk, and it's clear he's gone completely crazy.

The final shoot-out scene: Travis goes to rescue Iris from her life as a prostitute and goes blazing through a hotel, shooting people. At the end, he sits on the couch, covered in blood, surrounded by police; he's out of bullets and makes a gun out of his thumb and index finger, and pretends to shoot it at his own head. It is a chilling, disturbing, memorable image of someone who has completely lost it.

Travis takes Iris, the young prostitute, out to breakfast.

QUOTABLES

"You talkin' to me?"

Travis says this to himself in the mirror as he tests out a makeshift quick-draw gun harness that he has made. It turns into a whole monologue in which he acts out scenarios that lead to him pulling a gun on someone.

NETWORK

DIRECTOR: SIDNEY LUMET

SCREENWRITER: PADDY CHAYEFSKY

WHAT IT'S ABOUT

Howard Beale is a veteran anchor at a sinking news TV station, and his ratings are in the toilet. He gets fired and, in a farewell broadcast, tells viewers to tune in the following week when he'll kill himself on air. He persuades network bosses to let him on air one more time, just so he can bid his audience of many years a proper farewell, but ends up ranting against things like a bad economy, high oil prices, and pollution. The network is furious at first, but then they notice that the ratings have jumped, and beautiful and ambitious network executive Diana Christensen masterminds a plan to rehire Howard as "the mad prophet of the airwaves." Howard agrees, though his friend and fellow veteran journalist Max Schumacher doubts the integrity of the proposal and is concerned about Howard's mental health. Then, one evening on TV, Howard tells people to go to their windows and say, "I'm as mad as hell, and I'm not going to take this anymore!" (They do.) After this, he becomes a big-time radio personality who is part of a salacious news hour that also hosts gossip columnists and psychics.

Meanwhile, Diana and Max, despite their ethical differences (she cares about ratings, he cares about news) start having an affair that causes Max to leave his wife. But Diana can't love Max—she is too self-centered—and when Howard's ratings inevitably start sinking, Diana and Max split, and the network makes a decision to do something radical: They have Howard assassinated on public TV.

Who's In It

Faye Dunaway as Diana Christensen

William Holden as Max Schumacher

Peter Finch as Howard Beale

Beatrice Straight as Louise Schumacher

Robert Duvall as Frank Hackett

Ned Beatty as Arthur Jensen

More with Robert Duvall

The Godfather (1972, page 87)
Apocalypse Now (1979, page 129)
Tender Mercies (1983)
Sling Blade (1996)
The Apostle (1997)

WHY ALL THE FUSS?

The movie is a commentary on how some media executives will do anything for ratings (which equals money), even putting a suicidal crazy guy on the air. It is considered to be one of the best satires in movie history, while also tackling the subjects of ambition, exploitation, and greed.

Screenwriter Paddy Chayefsky took home the Oscar for the script.

It was ahead of its time and predicted "How low can you go?" reality television shows, such as the *Jerry Springer Show*, *Celebrity Rehab With Dr. Drew*, and *Rock of Love*.

The movie's performances are great. Faye Dunaway, Peter Finch, and Beatrice Straight all won Oscars, and both William Holden and Ned Beatty were nominated.

Bonus Material

★ Finch died before the Oscars and was the first actor to receive the award after death. (James Dean and Spencer Tracy had been nominated for posthumous awards as well but did not win.) Finch did live to see his nomination, though, and he was bitter that he was nominated for Best Supporting Actor, thinking his role was more worthy of Best Actor consideration.

★ Real-life newsman Walter Cronkite and actor Henry Fonda were both approached to play Howard Beale, but they turned down the role.

THE STUFF PEOPLE STILL TALK ABOUT

The dump scene: Max Schmuacher tells his wife of 25 years that he's leaving her for Diana. Beatrice Straight played Max's wife, and she was on screen for only 10 minutes. She won the Oscar for Best Supporting Actress—she's that good.

The "There is no America" scene: After Howard jeopardizes a big deal for the network, a television executive takes him into a dark conference room and explains in so many words that money makes the world go 'round. This is a precursor to another famous scene, in the 1987 movie *Wall Street*, in which mega-banker Gordon Gekko proclaims, "Greed is good."

Howard and his rants: Howard's thoughts on the dumbing down of Americans, their reliance on the TV, the corporate control of the airwaves, and more are frequently referenced or used. (One such example of this is in the 2007 controversial documentary *Zeitgeist*.)

Howard tells his TV audience to go to their windows and scream, "I'm as mad as hell, and I'm not going to take this anymore!"

QUOTABLES

"I'm as mad as hell, and I'm not going to take this anymore!"

Howard says this when he's on-air—a clear sign he's lost his mind—and then hundreds of people scream it out their windows. This line is now often referenced when people are fed up with a situation. (This movie is where it first came from.)

ALL THE PRESIDENT'S MEN
DIRECTOR: ALAN J. PAKULA
SCREENWRITER: WILLIAM GOLDMAN

WHAT IT'S ABOUT

All the President's Men tells the true story of how two young reporters from *The Washington Post* uncovered the presidential scandal known as Watergate. In this scandal, President Nixon and his Committee to Re-Elect the President were doing illegal things that included the misuse of campaign funds, and attempts to sabotage political opponents, and then covering up the truth about these activities. In a series of stories told over several months, Bob Woodward and Carl Bernstein reported on the scandal, and their work led to a criminal investigation that uncovered corruption that went all the way to the top—to the president. Ultimately, Nixon resigned.

All the President's Men is based on Bob Woodward and Carl Bernstein's 1974 book by the same name.

Who's In It

Dustin Hoffman as
Carl Bernstein

Robert Redford as
Bob Woodward

Hal Holbrook as
Deep Throat

Jason Robards as
Ben Bradlee

More With Dustin Hoffman

The Graduate (1967,
page 55)
Midnight Cowboy (1969)
Kramer vs. Kramer (1979)
Tootsie (1982)
Rain Man (1988)

More With Robert Redford

*Butch Cassidy and the
Sundance Kid* (1969)
The Way We Were (1973)
The Sting (1973)
The Natural (1984)
Out of Africa (1985)

WHY ALL THE FUSS?

Pretty much every TV show and film about newspapers that was made afterward has been somehow influenced by it, including *Think Broadcast News, The Wire, Shattered Glass, Good Night, and Good Luck.*, and *Zodiac.*

It was the first film that showed the real life of journalists: the long hours, arguments in the newsrooms, debates over what kind of news is important, and commitment to getting the facts out.

Even though audiences knew the outcome of *All the President's Men* and even though it was a movie about the relatively unsexy work of newspaper journalism, the film is exciting because every scene uncovers another clue that leads to the scandal getting blown wide open.

It's an accurate representation of one of the greatest political scandals in the history of the country.

Both Robert Redford and Dustin Hoffman received great reviews for their performances as the young journalists, and Jason Robards won the Oscar for his portrayal of the paper's executive editor.

Bonus Material

★ The movie was not shot in *The Washington Post* newsroom. Instead, a $450,000 replica was built in Los Angeles. Trash, papers, and desks from the *Post* offices were shipped to California to make it feel more real.

★ Frank Wills, the Watergate guard who discovered the initial break-in, plays himself in the film.

★ The identity of Deep Throat was a topic of much debate for decades, and Woodward swore he'd never tell, at least while his source was still alive. In 2005, an elderly Mark Felt, who was second in command at the FBI during the Nixon administration, came out as the mysterious inside man (a fact that Woodward confirmed).

THE STUFF PEOPLE STILL TALK ABOUT

Deep Throat: The confidential and very mysterious source who aided Bernstein and Woodward's investigation.

Woodstein: The nickname the executive editor gave to the pair of young reporters.

The bugging scene: After Deep Throat has told Woodward that his and Bernstein's lives might be in danger, Woodward goes to Bernstein's apartment, turns music up loud (to foil any attempts to bug the room), and types out a message on Bernstein's typewriter explaining the high stakes.

The reporting: Woodward and Bernstein interview countless people, showing up at sources' houses late at night, chatting for hours over coffee while trying to seem non-threatening, and furiously taking notes during phone conversations. The movie does a good job of portraying how much legwork goes into reporting a big story.

Bernstein and Woodward going over their notes in the newsroom.

QUOTABLES

"Follow the money."

A confidential source nicknamed Deep Throat says this to Bernstein in the dark bowels of a parking garage. The line indicated that financial records would lead to the guilty parties.

ROCKY

DIRECTOR: JOHN G. AVILDSEN

SCREENWRITER: SYLVESTER STALLONE

WHAT IT'S ABOUT

Rocky Balboa is a past-his-prime boxer in Philadelphia who now makes cash as a debt collector for a loan shark. He still fights small-time matches, but pretty much everyone thinks he's washed up. Apollo Creed, the heavyweight champion of the world, comes to town and, as a publicity stunt, proposes the idea of giving a local nobody the shot of fighting him. Creed takes a liking to Rocky's nickname "The Italian Stallion" and has the fight promoter ask Rocky to participate. Rocky agrees to the match, believing it's a once-in-a-lifetime opportunity.

Rocky is out of shape, and his former trainer, Mickey, who had written him off, signs on to be his manager and help him prepare for the fight. Through intense training that consists of early-morning runs, intense workouts with Mickey, and using carcasses at the local meat factory as punching bags, Rocky prepares for the high-profile showdown. Along the way, he hooks up with Adrian, a painfully shy woman who works at a pet store. No one, from Creed to Rocky himself, expects Rocky to make it through the fight, but what starts out as a publicity stunt quickly becomes an all-out bloody throw-down. Rocky doesn't come out the winner, but he does show everyone he's certainly not the loser they thought him to be.

Who's In It

Sylvester Stallone as
Rocky Balboa

Burgess Meredith as
Mickey Goldmill

Talia Shire as
Adrian Pennino

Burt Young as
Paulie Pennino

Carl Weathers as
Apollo Creed

More With
Sylvester Stallone

Rocky II-V (1979-90)
First Blood (1982)
Cliffhanger (1993)
The Specialist (1994)
Cop Land (1997)

WHY ALL THE FUSS?

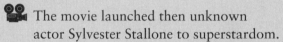
The movie perfectly paints a picture of its scrappy and determined working-class hero and his friends. And, while some may consider it cheesy, it's a classic inspirational story of heart, grit, and love. Rocky overcomes incredible odds through lots of hard work, determination, the support of his friends, and the love of a good woman.

The movie launched then unknown actor Sylvester Stallone to superstardom.

★ Stallone wrote *Rocky* in less than four days, and the total shooting budget was a low $960,000, but it became the year's top-grossing film.

★ As screenwriter, Stallone had decided that he would sell the script only if he could play the lead role. Luckily, United Artists bought it and allowed him to do just that.

Rocky rests a moment during a fight, with Mickey, his manager, at his side.

THE STUFF PEOPLE STILL TALK ABOUT

The pre-fight montage: Backed by the now-famous theme song "Gonna Fly Now" (composed by Bill Conti), Rocky trains by running through the streets of Philadelphia, pounding animal carcasses at the meat-packing factory, doing one-armed pushups at his low-budget boxing gym, and finally running up the steps of the Philadelphia Museum of Art, where he raises his fists in triumph. (Earlier in the movie, he is unable to make it to the top of the steps because he's out of shape.)

Burgess Meredith's performance: He is equally tough and heartbreaking as Mickey, the crusty boxing coach and veteran.

The final fight scene: Rocky delivers a performance no one expected of him, but not without a lot of blood and sweat.

QUOTABLES

"Yo, Adrian!"

Rocky says this as a shout-out to his girlfriend during a television appearance; it sounds Neanderthal, but he says it with such love that it's actually pretty sweet.

1977 ANNIE HALL
DIRECTOR: WOODY ALLEN
SCREENWRITERS: WOODY ALLEN AND MARSHALL BRICKMAN

WHAT IT'S ABOUT

Loopy, paranoid Jewish comedian Alvy Singer meets ditsy photographer-singer Annie and they fall in—and out—of love against the backdrop of New York City. Alvy narrates the movie, as he tries to figure out what went wrong in his relationship with Annie. He also mulls over his past relationships with other women—including his loud, critical mother. The movie chronicles the couple's relationship from their meeting at a tennis match to their happy courtship, strained sex life (he wants it more than she does), and fights (usually about sex). Through absurd flashbacks, present-day Alvy and Annie watch Annie's past interactions with her old boyfriends and Alvy in a previous relationship in which he avoids sex by talking about Kennedy assassination conspiracies. (The flashbacks also show clips of Alvy as a young child explaining that he's depressed because "the universe is expanding.")

Alvy is convinced that it will help his and Annie's relationship if she sees a therapist, so she does—but it only helps her realize how unhappy she is in her life with him. Eventually, Annie moves to California to pursue a career as a singer. She and Alvy remain friends, but he is left to his own seemingly hopeless devices on the lonely streets of New York.

Who's In It

Woody Allen as Alvy Singer

Diane Keaton as Annie Hall

Tony Roberts as Rob

Carol Kane as Allison

Shelley Duvall as Pam

More Written by Woody Allen

Sleeper (1973)
Manhattan (1979)
Zelig (1983)
Hannah and Her Sisters (1986)
Mighty Aphrodite (1995)
Vicky Cristina Barcelona (2008)

More With Diane Keaton

The Godfather (1972, page 87)
Looking for Mr. Goodbar (1977)
Father of the Bride (1991)
Something's Gotta Give (2003)

WHY ALL THE FUSS?

Woody Allen combined humor, neurosis, and intellectualism to illustrate the human condition in a way no one had seen before. This is also the movie in which he established the pop culture archetype of the brainy, neurotic Jewish New Yorker.

Diane Keaton as Annie became known as the quintessential urban scatter-brained heroine. Her character's wardrobe of baggy pants, men's shirts, ties, vests, and bowler hat became known as the Annie Hall Look. She also won the Best Actress Oscar for her performance.

Allen tried a whole bunch of new techniques to tell the movie's story, like having characters directly address the camera and using split screens, subtitles, animation, and flashbacks at random and unexpected moments.

Annie Hall got Oscars for Best Director, Best Screenplay, and Best Picture (beating out *Star Wars*!).

QUOTABLES

"There's a spider in your bathroom the size of a Buick."
Alvy says this to Annie when she calls him over to her house to kill a bug.

"I would never want to belong to any club that would have someone like me for a member."
Alvy quotes Groucho Marx when he is analyzing why his relationships with women fail. (Anyone who likes him must be a loser.)

THE STUFF PEOPLE STILL TALK ABOUT

The lobster scene: Alvy and Annie are at a summer house and are about to boil lobsters for dinner, and chaos ensues when a lobster crawls behind the fridge.

The Marshall McLuhan scene: Alvy is in line at the movies and some arrogant guy behind him is blathering on about something media critic Marshall McLuhan said. Alvy turns to McLuhan (who is suddenly and magically standing next to him in the lobby) and listens while McLuhan tells the loudmouth he has no understanding of his work. It's a very funny revenge fantasy.

The roller-coaster clip: Alvy claims that he grew up literally under a roller coaster in Brooklyn, New York, and an onscreen image depicts just that.

★ The movie was initially titled *Anhedonia*, which is Greek for "the incapacity for pleasure."

★ In a Central Park scene, Alvy and Annie are people-watching and Alvy describes a person by saying: "There's the winner of the Truman Capote look-alike contest." The "actor" in the scene is in fact Capote himself!

★ Allen's first choice for the person to shut down the pompous jerk in the movie line scene was film-maker Federico Fellini. Marshall McLuhan was ultimately cast.

★ Prior to directing *Annie Hall*, Allen was known for making silly comedies, such as *Bananas* and *Sleeper*, but *Annie Hall* made him a household name.

Annie and Alvy on the streets of New York City.

1977

SATURDAY NIGHT FEVER

DIRECTOR: JOHN BADHAM

SCREENWRITER: NORMAN WEXLER

WHAT IT'S ABOUT

Tony Manero is a 19-year-old guy from Bay Ridge, Brooklyn, who works in a hardware store during the week and is a dancing star at disco 2001 Odyssey on Saturday nights. Tony's not exactly on the fast track to success, and he still lives with his parents and hangs out with his old friends from the neighborhood. He enters the disco's dance contest with his insecure friend Annette (who clearly has a crush on him) but drops her when he meets Stephanie, a talented dancer who works in Manhattan as a secretary and aspires to the sophisticated ways of the big city. The two have great chemistry on the dance floor, but Tony is drawn to Stephanie in a romantic way, and she's not interested in being with him.

The night of the dance contest, Tony and Stephanie dance well, but the last couple to dance blows them off the deck; Tony and Stephanie win anyway, but Tony gives the trophy to the other couple, feeling they deserved it more. After the dance, Tony comes on to Stephanie really hard, but she rejects him and leaves. So he hangs out with his old buddies that night, which ends with one depressed friend falling to his death—perhaps intentionally—off the Verrazano-Narrows Bridge. Tony then realizes he needs to move beyond his life in Brooklyn, and Stephanie is the one person in his life who is interested in making it outside the borough. He heads to her apartment in Manhattan, hoping to start fresh with her, as friends, and start a new life of his own.

Who's In It

John Travolta as
Tony Manero

Karen Lynn Gorney as
Stephanie

Barry Miller as
Bobby C.

Donna Pescow as
Annette

Joseph Cali as Joey

More With
John Travolta

Grease (1978)
Urban Cowboy (1980)
Pulp Fiction (1994)
Hairspray (2007)

WHY ALL THE FUSS?

Saturday Night Fever is the movie that brought disco into the mainstream and is now a symbol of the disco era.

It was a huge hit when it came out, and the soundtrack, made up of songs primarily by disco trio the Bee Gees, produced a whole bunch of chart-toppers, including "Staying Alive."

John Travolta has made a ton of movies, but Tony Manero is one of his most famous roles; he will always be that guy in the white polyester suit.

Saturday Night Fever is based on a 1976 *New York Magazine* cover story by Nik Cohn titled "Tribal Rites of the New Saturday Night."

Bonus Material

★ *Saturday Night Fever* was film critic Gene Siskel's favorite movie. He not only saw it 17 times, but also bought the iconic white suit at a charity auction.

★ The information in the article on which the movie was based— "Tribal Rites of the New Saturday Night"—was made up, writer Nik Cohn later admitted.

★ The dance floor (see next page) at 2001 Odyssey, the Brooklyn club where the dancing scenes were shot, was custom-built for the movie and cost $15,000. It was auctioned off when the club, later renamed Spectrum, closed in 2005.

★ The movie has been referenced or parodied in loads of places, including *The Simpsons*, *Family Guy*, *Airplane!* (page 132), *Sesame Street Fever*, and Madonna's "Hung Up" music video.

THE STUFF PEOPLE STILL TALK ABOUT

The opening sequence: Tony is strutting down the street on his way to the hardware store, as "Staying Alive" plays in the background.

The dance floor: It's multicolored and lights up.

The dance scenes: They showcase disco dancing (for better or worse), 1970s outfits, 1970s hair, and elaborate dance moves that now look really outdated and goofy, such as the line dance the Hustle.

The dance floor image: Tony (a very young John Travolta) strikes a pose (one arm pointing up, the other pointing down) on a multicolored dance floor wearing a tight white suit.

Stephanie and Tony out on the dance floor, as Tony strikes his famous pose.

QUOTABLES

"Would you just watch the hair?"

Tony, who is prepped to go out dancing, says this to his father after his father hits the side of Tony's head at the dinner table. It's ridiculous and funny, but also shows how serious Tony is about his life at the disco.

1978 SUPERMAN

DIRECTOR: RICHARD DONNER

SCREENWRITERS: MARIO PUZO, DAVID NEWMAN, LESLIE NEWMAN, AND ROBERT BENTON

WHAT IT'S ABOUT

Baby Kal-El is sent to Earth by his parents in a giant white space pod when his home planet of Krypton is destroyed. The Kents, a nice couple in Kansas who come across him when driving down a country road, adopt him and name him Clark. They soon discover he's ... kind of special. He can run faster than a speeding train, kick a ball miles, and, even as a baby, lift a truck on his own.

One day, Clark finds a glowing crystal in the family barn, which leads him to an ice palace where he learns about who he is. He then moves to the big city of Metropolis and disguises himself as a dorky, fumbling newspaper reporter for *The Daily Planet*. He meets fellow *Planet* journalist Lois Lane and starts to have a thing for her. But while he's a mild-mannered reporter by day, he's a caped crusader at night, foiling robberies and saving lives. Soon, villain Lex Luthor makes a plan to destroy much of the West Coast (and Hackensack, New Jersey), and Superman must take him down. He succeeds, but Lex's plan causes Lois to be in a fatal accident, and Superman—in a hard decision—decides to bring her back to life. Luthor is captured and sent to prison, and back at the office Lois has no idea that the dorky Clark actually saved her.

Superman was inspired by the hugely popular DC comic book series of the same name.

Who's In It

Christopher Reeve as Superman/Clark Kent

Margot Kidder as Lois Lane

Marlon Brando as Jor-El

Gene Hackman as Lex Luthor

Jackie Cooper as Perry White

Ned Beatty as Otis

More With Christopher Reeve

Superman II (1980)
Somewhere in Time (1980)
Deathtrap (1982)
The Remains of the Day (1993)
Rear Window
(TV remake, 1998, page 121 for the original)

WHY ALL THE FUSS?

It is the grand-daddy of the modern superhero movie. Without *Superman*, there is no *Spider-Man*, no *Batman*, no *Iron Man*.

It was a big-budget film with break-through special effects. The movie's tag line was "You'll believe a man can fly!" and that was, in fact, the case. (The film won a Special Achievement Award for visual effects at that year's Oscars.)

The film introduced then-unknown actor Christopher Reeve. He was universally praised as embodying both the Man of Steel and the awkward Clark Kent.

It proved that superhero movies weren't just for kids anymore, and that they could be huge box office successes.

QUOTABLES

Superman: "I've got you."
Lois: "You've got me! Who's got you!?"
The exchange between Lois Lane and Superman, as they fly away
after he's saved her from falling off a skyscraper.

"Miss Teschmacher!"
Lex Luthor repeatedly yells out the name of his female companion
throughout the movie. It's sort of his catchphrase.

THE STUFF PEOPLE STILL TALK ABOUT

Superman takes Lois for a romantic flight.

The breakthrough special effects: It really looked like Superman was flying.

The romantic flight scene: Superman stops by Lois's penthouse apartment for an exclusive interview; after the chat, they end up cruising through the sky together. During the flight, there's a very cheesy "Can you read my mind?" voice-over monologue performed by the totally smitten Lois.

John William's score: The victorious, uplifting orchestral music of the movie not only makes you believe a man can fly, but also that, maybe, *you* can fly.

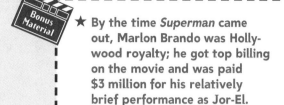

★ By the time *Superman* came out, Marlon Brando was Hollywood royalty; he got top billing on the movie and was paid $3 million for his relatively brief performance as Jor-El.

★ Other actors considered for the role of *Superman* were Warren Beatty and Nick Nolte.

★ Much of what would become the movie's sequel—*Superman II*—was shot by director Richard Donner during the production of *Superman*, but after hearing creative differences with the second film's producers, he was fired and replaced by Richard Lester, who completed the sequel.

★ The 2006 movie *Superman Returns* includes many references to the 1978 original.

★ Christopher Reeve was paralyzed in a horseback riding accident in 1995 and spent the rest of his life helping and advocating for people with disabilities.

LEGENDARY OSCAR MOMENTS

Established in 1929, the Academy Awards ceremony—or Oscars, as it's often called—recognizes the highest achievements in filmmaking. It's held annually by the Academy of Motion Picture Arts and Sciences (AMPAS). These are some of the juiciest moments from past ceremonies.

★ In 1939, Hattie McDaniel is named Best Supporting Actress for her role in *Gone With the Wind* (page 14) and becomes the first African-American to win an Oscar.

★ Also in 1939, the Oscar winners were leaked to *The Los Angeles Times* before the ceremony happened and printed in the paper's early edition before they were announced. As a result, today only an accounting firm knows the results prior to the show.

★ In 1968, Katharine Hepburn and Barbra Streisand tied for Best Actress for their roles in *The Lion in Winter* and *Funny Girl*, respectively. This was a first for the Oscars.

★ In 1974, a man named Robert Opal interrupted the ceremony by running across the stage naked—a fad at the time known as streaking—and flashing a peace sign. He was caught and taken to the pressroom for photos.

★ In 1984, Sally Field won the Oscar for Best Actress and delivered what would become the most quoted line from the awards: "You like me! Right now, you like me!"

★ In 1986, Cher made Oscar headlines not for her acting, but for her outrageous outfit by designer Bob Mackie: It was a black belly-baring, sequin- and feather-adorned dress, topped off by a huge feather headpiece.

★ In 1992, 72-year-old actor Jack Palance won Best Supporting Actor for his role in *City Slickers* after decades of working in Hollywood; to celebrate, he dropped to the floor and did three one-armed push-ups.

★ In 1996, Cuba Gooding Jr. won the Best Supporting Actor Oscar for his role in *Jerry Maguire*. He delivered a hyper, joy-filled acceptance speech, proclaiming "I love you! I love you! I love you!" and brought the entire audience to its feet.

- ★ In 1998, *Titanic* director James Cameron won Best Director (the movie picked up 11 Oscars in all that night). As part of his acceptance speech, he quotes the film's main character, Jack Dawson, by proclaiming, "I'm the king of the world!" He comes across as an egomaniac, but then again his movie had just won 11 Oscars and was the biggest-grossing film of all time.

- ★ In 1999, upon winning Best Foreign Film for *Life Is Beautiful*, director and star of the film Roberto Benigni—a person known for his somewhat goofy personality—excitedly and joyfully jumped onto the back of a seat and climbed over Steven Spielberg to get to the stage.

- ★ In 2001, Halle Berry is named Best Actress for her performance in *Monster's Ball*, making her the first African-American woman in the history of the Oscars to win the award. She delivers a moving, tear-filled acceptance speech, in which she names the many actresses of color who came before her.

- ★ In 2003, actor Adrien Brody won Best Actor for his performance in *The Pianist*, an accomplishment that made him the youngest man to ever win the award. He went up on stage and planted a passionate kiss onto the award's presenter—the very beautiful (and very shocked, but understanding) Halle Berry.

WHY ARE THEY CALLED OSCARS?

Amazingly, no one really knows for sure. The most-repeated story goes that, in the early '30s, an AMPAS librarian named Margaret Herrick (she later became the executive director) felt the statue looked like her Uncle Oscar, and, as a result, the staff started calling it that. The nickname was popular enough that in 1934, a Hollywood columnist wrote about Katharine Hepburn winning the "Oscar" for Best Actress. By 1939, the Academy was using the nickname officially.

ANIMAL HOUSE

DIRECTOR: JOHN LANDIS

SCREENWRITERS: HAROLD RAMIS, DOUGLAS KENNEY, AND CHRIS MILLER

WHAT IT'S ABOUT

It's 1962, and Larry Kroger and Kent Dorfman are two freshmen trying to join a fraternity at Faber College. They first try to mingle with the snooty Omega Theta Pi frat but are strongly rejected. They then meet the Delta Tau Chi frat next door and find a much different scene. The house is a beer-soaked mess, and members of the fraternity include D-Day, who rides his motorcycle up the stairs, and Bluto, a loud, crass guy who's been in college for seven years. Larry and Kent become part of the fraternity.

But the dean of the school, Vernon Wormer, hates the Delta frat and wants to kick them off the campus. So he enlists the Omega frat boys to help him do that, and the Omegas figure out a way to seriously ruin the Deltas' GPAs. In response, the Deltas throw a massive toga party, complete with costumes made out of bed sheets, lots of beer, dancing, and hooking up. One member even spends the night with Wormer's wife. All of this and more causes the dean to finally revoke the Delta's charter and, eventually, expel them. In a final act of defiance, the Deltas bring chaos to the Homecoming Parade with a black "Deathmobile." The final minutes of the film let the audience know what became of the main characters—Bluto, of course, becomes a United States senator.

Animal House **is based on stories that Chris Miller had written for** *National Lampoon,* **a popular 1970s college humor magazine.**

Who's In It

John Belushi as John "Bluto" Blutarsky

Tom Hulce as Larry "Pinto" Kroger

Stephen Furst as Kent "Flounder" Dorfman

Tim Matheson as Eric Stratton

John Vernon as Dean Vernon Wormer

Peter Riegert as Donald Schoenstein

Bruce McGill as Daniel Simpson "D-Day" Day

More With John Belushi

Saturday Night Live, the TV series (1975–1979)
The Blues Brothers (1980)
Neighbors (1981)

WHY ALL THE FUSS?

📷 *Animal House* is credited with inventing the "gross-out" genre—films that feature disgusting, lewd, and juvenile gags. (There's lots of crass talk, drinking, women in various states of undress, and a very famous impression of an exploding zit.) It paved the way for flicks like *Porky's*, the Police Academy movies, *American Pie*, *Revenge of the Nerds*, and even *Jackass*.

📷 It's really funny. John Belushi's performance as the disgusting, offensive, and often drunk Bluto is unforgettable.

📷 Made for less than $3 million, it went on to gross more than $140 million; it became a phenomenon, and almost every college kid in America went to see it.

📷 It's an underdog story, pitting the snobby upper crust against a bunch of misfits and captures a classic portrait of college life in which kids are boozy, silly, sexed-up, and into pranks.

Bluto takes a look beneath the skirts of some cheerleaders.

Bonus Material

★ "Pinto" was writer Chris Miller's nickname in college.

★ The film was shot at the University of Oregon.

★ The horse that is snuck into the dean's office was, in fact, snuck into the University of Oregon's dean's office to film the scene.

★ A very young Kevin Bacon plays the snotty Omega pledge Chip Diller.

THE STUFF PEOPLE STILL TALK ABOUT

The zit scene: Bluto does his impression of an exploding zit by eating a glob of mashed potatoes and then squishing his cheeks together—spraying the contents of his mouth all over rivals from the Omega frat.

The "Shout" scene: At the Delta's wild toga party, Otis Day & the Knights perform this song and everyone boogies down.

Bluto's can-crushing: Bluto has a habit of flattening beer cans on his head.

The guitar smash scene: A guy is playing a sappy love song for girls at the toga party when Bluto walks by, listens, takes the guitar out of the guy's hands, and smashes it to bits against the wall.

D-Day's "William Tell Overture": D-Day makes his entrance by storming up the stairs inside the Delta frat house on his motorcycle and "playing" the "William Tell Overture" on his throat.

QUOTABLES

"To-ga! To-ga!"
Bluto almost reflexively starts to chant this when it's suggested that the Deltas throw a toga party, and the rest of the guys eventually join in.

"Food fight!"
Bluto yells this after he's done his zit impression and it starts an all-out food war. (People now yell this when an actual food fight is taking place.)

"Then as of this moment, they're on DOUBLE SECRET PROBATION!"
Dean Wormer resorts to this when he learns that the Deltas can't be put on probation because they already are.

APOCALYPSE NOW

DIRECTOR: FRANCIS FORD COPPOLA

SCREENWRITERS: JOHN MILIUS AND FRANCIS FORD COPPOLA

WHAT IT'S ABOUT

It's the Vietnam War, and Captain Benjamin Willard is a seasoned vet who's been hanging out in Saigon waiting for an assignment. But when he gets his next set of orders, it's not what he expects: He's directed to head into the deep jungles of Cambodia on a top-secret mission to kill Colonel Kurtz, a once-decorated soldier who has gone completely bonkers and is now serving as the leader of a cultlike community of Cambodian jungle natives.

Captian Willard sets off, along with an unsuspecting group of soldiers, on a deadly, insanity-inducing journey upriver that includes encounters with warrior/surfer Colonel Bill Kilgore, enemy fire, some Playboy bunnies (brought in to entertain troops), and even a tiger. The men try to maintain some sense of normalcy, but the combination of death, fear, and uncertainty drives all of them at least a little crazy. With half of his crew dead, Willard finally arrives at Kurtz's compound and finds a horrific scene of brain-washed followers and decapitated heads. He meets with Kurtz, a bald, delusional leader who commands his people from a dark, dank room and is well aware of Willard's deadly intentions. In the end, Kurtz allows Willard to kill him, but not before sharing his thoughts on man's capacity for evil.

Apocalypse Now* is based on Joseph Conrad's 1902 novella *Heart of Darkness.

Who's In It

Martin Sheen as
Captain Benjamin L. Willard

Marlon Brando as
Colonel Walter E. Kurtz

Robert Duvall as
Lieutenant Colonel Bill Kilgore

Albert Hall as
George Phillips

Frederic Forrest as
Jay "Chef" Hicks

Laurence Fishburne as
Tyrone 'Clean' Miller

Harrison Ford as
Colonel Lucas

Dennis Hopper as
Photojournalist

More Directed by Francis Ford Coppola

The Godfather (1972, page 87)
The Conversation (1974)
The Godfather II (1974)
The Outsiders (1983)
Rumble Fish (1983)

WHY ALL THE FUSS?

- *Apocalypse Now* is considered to be one of the best films about the Vietnam War, ever. It captures the hell of war and the particularly miserable, paranoia-inducing aspects of the Vietnam conflict (fear of enemies hiding in the jungle waiting to attack, intense humidity, and not knowing who to trust).

- It explores some very dark issues of human nature and insanity.

- Marlon Brando's and Robert Duvall's performances as the unhinged Kurtz and the blood-thirsty Colonel Kilgore, respectively, were highly acclaimed.

- *Apocalypse Now* is a precursor to anti-war films such as *Platoon* and *Full Metal Jacket*; it is considered an especially powerful anti-war movie because it shows how war, in general, reflects humanity's dark side.

Bonus Material

★ Despite the props it garnered, the filming of *Apocalypse Now* was something of a disaster. Coppola contemplated suicide at one point, Sheen suffered a heart attack during filming, and Brando, whose character was supposed to be gaunt from spending so many years in the jungle, arrived on the set fat. (All of this and more is documented in the film *Hearts of Darkness: A Filmmaker's Apocalypse*, which is about the making of the movie.)

★ Sheen was not first choice for the part of Captain Willard. Jack Nicholson, Robert Redford, Gene Hackman, Al Pacino, and James Caan were all offered the part—and turned it down.

★ Actors with smaller roles in the film who went on to become major stars include Harrison Ford, Laurence Fishburne, and Dennis Hopper.

THE STUFF PEOPLE STILL TALK ABOUT

The opening sequence: A troubled Willard, haunted by his experience fighting in Vietnam and waiting in a Saigon hotel room for his next assignment, drinks himself into a stupor, and ends up naked on the floor crying and bleeding (after hitting a mirror) with the Doors' song, "The End" playing on the soundtrack.

"The Ride of the Valkyries" bombing scene: American helicopters led by Colonel Kilgore descend upon and destroy a Vietnamese village while German composer Richard Wagner's "The Ride of the Valkyries" plays in the background. The music is threatening and loud and the effect is chilling, as we watch villagers shoot at the helicopters and run for their lives. Once on the ground, Kilgore becomes obsessed with taking advantage of prime surfing waves as the battle rages around him

Willard arrives at Kurtz's compound to find a horrific scene.

QUOTABLES

"I love the smell of napalm in the morning."

Colonel Kilgore says this to Captain Willard after the US bombed a Vietnamese village, showing how insensitive he has become to forces of destruction.
(Napalm is gelled gasoline that is often used in warfare.)

"The horror... the horror."

These are Colonel Kurtz's last, haunting words.

AIRPLANE!

DIRECTORS: JIM ABRAHAMS AND DAVID ZUCKER

SCREENWRITERS: JIM ABRAHAMS, DAVID ZUCKER, AND JERRY ZUCKER

WHAT IT'S ABOUT

Former Navy pilot Ted Striker boards the plane of stewardess Elaine Dickinson, who's recently dumped him, in an effort to get her back. A meal of bad fish causes many passengers (and more important, the entire flight crew) to fall gravely ill, and although (an inflatable) automatic pilot can fly the plane, it can't land it. Ted is the only person left on board who might be able to do that, but he has a serious phobia of flying, due to the fact that he lost several men as the captain of a crew in the war.

In the cabin, some passengers freak out and others try to calm themselves by singing, drinking, or doing drugs. Back on the ground, a harried group of air-traffic controllers attempts to bring the plane in safely. Ted does try to fly the plane but succumbs to the stress and chickens out. Eventually, he musters the courage to land the plane, and Elaine is at his side as his copilot as they bring the plane in safely.

The script was a spoof on a 1957 dramatic movie *Zero Hour*.

Who's In It

Robert Hays as
Ted Striker

Julie Hagerty as
Elaine Dickinson

Lloyd Bridges as
Steve McCroskey

Leslie Nielsen as
Dr. Rumack

Robert Stack as
Rex Kramer

Peter Graves as Captain
Clarence Oveur

Kareem Abdul-Jabbar
as Roger Murdock

More With
Leslie Nielsen

*The Naked Gun: From the
Files of Police Squad!* (1988)
*The Naked Gun 2 1/2:
The Smell of Fear* (1991)
Spy Hard (1996)
Scary Movie 3 (2003)

WHY ALL THE FUSS?

It pretty much invented the spoof movie category, poking fun at the many 1970s disaster movies that had been put out that decade. One example of *Airplane!*'s influence is the entire Scary Movie franchise, which would not exist without *Airplane!*

Airplane! included in its cast several of the very same actors (such as Robert Stack, Peter Graves, and Leslie Nielsen) who had appeared in the popular disaster movies of the 1970s; the joke was that these actors performed their roles with the same seriousness they had in dramatic films in the past—but this movie was a comedy.

Ultimately, what makes *Airplane!* such a hilarious and truly great movie is its gags, like an automatic pilot that is an inflatable doll of a guy in a pilot's uniform; a ground-control employee who unplugs the runway lights (and then says "just kidding" and plugs them back in); and the many verbal jokes in which people takes things extremely literally.

Ted takes control of the plane with the help of Elaine and the inflatable automatic pilot.

Bonus Material

★ The woman who translates jive talk is Barbara Billingsley, the actress who played an all-American mom, June Cleaver, in the 1950s TV series *Leave It to Beaver*.

★ The movie contains the last appearance on film of show biz legend Ethel Merman. She plays a shell-shocked male soldier who thinks he's Ethel Merman. Her previous films include *There's No Business Like Show Business* and *It's a Mad, Mad, Mad, Mad World*.

THE STUFF PEOPLE STILL TALK ABOUT

The old lady jive talker: At one point in the movie, a very proper-looking older woman steps forward to translate the jive talk of two black passengers.

The passenger flip-out scene: Passengers line up to smack a woman who is freaking out about the plane crashing. They are carrying weapons such as a gun, a baseball bat, and boxing gloves.

The comedy of names: There are frequent hilarious exchanges among the flight crew, based on their names of Roger, Clarence Oveur, and Victor; it's a newer take on the classic Abbot and Costello routine: "Who's on Fifth?" Examples: "We have clearance Clarence" "What's our vector, Victor?" "Roger, Roger."

QUOTABLES

"I am serious ... and don't call me Shirley."
Dr. Rumack to Ted, after Ted has said, "Surely, you can't be serious."

"Looks like I picked the wrong week to quit smoking."
The stressed-out Steve McCroskey, who lights a cigarette and proceeds to pick up other addictions—like sniffing glue—as the night continues.

Elaine: "You got a letter from headquarters this morning."
Ted: "What is it?"
Elaine: "It's a big building where generals meet, but that's not important."
Just one of the taking-it-too-literally bits of dialogue in the movie.

1980

THE SHINING
DIRECTOR: STANLEY KUBRICK
SCREENWRITER: STANLEY KUBRICK

WHAT IT'S ABOUT

The Shining starts when recovering alcoholic and writer Jack Torrance takes a job as the winter caretaker of the sprawling and remote Overlook Hotel and brings along his wife, Wendy, and young son, Danny. He soon learns the job drove one man to total madness, perhaps due to the extreme isolation, and that the man had killed his wife and young daughters. Before leaving for the winter, the resident cook has a telepathic conversation with Danny and realizes that the boy has a psychic gift (called "the shining").

Danny's psychic gift allows him to detect the ghostly presences in the hotel, and he begins to have horrific visions of blood-filled elevators and creepy-looking sisters. As snow piles up outside, Jack is driven mad by the ghosts in the hotel (he sees a beautiful naked woman turn into an old, sagging corpse, and listens to ghostly hotel employees who convince him it is necessary to murder his wife and son). Both Danny and Jack are seemingly haunted by the tormented spirits that still reside at Overlook. Eventually, Wendy decides to look at the manuscript Jack has supposedly been working on the whole time, and she is horrified to find that it is all gibberish. When she confronts him, Jack reveals he's intentionally stranded her and Danny there with him.

Who's In It

Jack Nicholson as
Jack Torrance

Shelley Duvall as
Wendy Torrance

Danny Lloyd as
Danny Torrance

Scatman Crothers as
Dick Hallorann

Joe Turkel as
Lloyd the Bartender

More With Jack Nicholson

Easy Rider (1969, page 70)
Five Easy Pieces (1970)
Chinatown (1974)
One Flew Over the Cuckoo's Nest (1975)
Terms of Endearment (1983)
As Good as It Gets (1997)

The Shining is based on Stephen King's 1977 novel by the same name.

WHY ALL THE FUSS?

 Director Stanley Kubrick creates a creepy and claustrophobic world at the remote, snowed-in Overlook, with images of seriously disturbing stuff, like a tidal wave of blood spilling out of an elevator and a pair of zombie-like little girls who appear out of nowhere from time to time.

 Jack Nicholson's performance as a normal guy turned murderous madman is convincing, to say the least. It gave lots of kids nightmares for years.

 Kubrick used something called a Steadicam—a device that attaches the camera to a cameraperson's body in a way that allows the cameraperson to follow a subject freely while also producing a totally smooth and steady shot. (As opposed to a handheld camera, which even when used well, can produce choppy and jarring shots.) Kubrick used the then-innovative tool to follow Danny as he rode around the halls of the hotel on his tricycle. The results were long, smooth, uninterrupted motion shots that hadn't been seen before.

 It is a rare example of when a movie inspired by a book may actually be even better than its source.

★ Both the bands 30 Seconds to Mars and Slipknot made videos based on the movie, filled with references to famous scenes and images.

★ Both *The Simpsons* and *Family Guy* have featured episodes inspired by *The Shining*.

★ Despite the film's success, Stephen King was not pleased with it and later wrote a screenplay for a TV movie of his novel, which aired in 1997 and didn't do nearly as well as the 1980 version.

THE STUFF PEOPLE STILL TALK ABOUT

Jack's insanity speech: After Wendy has discovered her husband's nonsensical manuscript and decides to leave right away with Danny, a crazy and possessed Jack stalks her up a flight of stairs, advising her finally that he's going to "bash her brains in."

"All work and no play makes Jack a dull boy": The phrase that Jack has written thousands of times while he's been claiming to work on his manuscript. (Turns out, he hasn't been working at all.)

The creepy girls: The sisters who were murdered years before and keep mysteriously appearing before Danny at the end of a hall.

Wendy tries to talk to a quickly unraveling Jack.

QUOTABLES

"Heeeere's Johnny!"
Jack says this to Wendy after axing his way through the bathroom door.

"Redrum."
Danny repeats this "nonsense" over and over one night until he wakes up Wendy—who, with the help of a mirror, discovers it's "murder" spelled backwards. Everyone pretty much knows what "Redrum" means today, but at the time it was a big surprise.

1981

RAIDERS OF THE LOST ARK

DIRECTOR: STEVEN SPIELBERG

SCREENWRITERS: GEORGE LUCAS, LAWRENCE KASDAN, AND PHILIP KAUFMAN

WHAT IT'S ABOUT

Archeology professor Indiana Jones (aka Indy) leads something of a double life. Some days, he's wearing a tweed suit and lecturing to adoring students; other days, he's traveling the globe in search of ancient artifacts—and potentially getting chased or shot at by people such as natives, enemies of the US, or professional rivals.

In the movie, which is set in 1936, Indy is approached by the US government to help stop the Nazis from finding the Ark of the Covenant, an ancient artifact said to contain the original Ten Commandments given to Moses. (Yes, the actual stone tablets.) Word is that any army that possesses the ark is undefeatable, which is why the Nazis want it so badly. Indy sets off on a dangerous, thrilling hunt to stop the Nazis; he makes his way from Nepal to Egypt and beyond. Along the way, he solves ancient puzzles and encounters tombs full of snakes and bodies, as well as numerous people who want to kill him. He also meets up with an old flame, Marion, who insists on coming along for the ride. Eventually, the Ark is indeed found, and despite changing hands several times, it ends up with the Nazis, who, in a final scene full of fire, melting faces, and the apparent wrath of God, come to understand the Ark's power a little too well.

Who's In It

Harrison Ford as
Indiana Jones

Karen Allen as
Marion Ravenwood

Paul Freeman as
Dr. Rene Belloq

Ronald Lacey as
Major Arnold Toht

John Rhys-Davies as
Sallah

Denholm Elliott as
Dr. Marcus Brody

More Directed by Steven Spielberg

Jaws (1975, page 94)
Close Encounters of the Third Kind (1977)
E.T.: The Extra-Terrestrial (1982)
Jurassic Park (1993)
Saving Private Ryan (1998)

WHY ALL THE FUSS?

It's the quintessential action flick, and one of the most entertaining movies ever made. The fact that it was a collaboration between *Star Wars* creator George Lucas and *Jaws* and *Close Encounters of the Third Kind* director Steven Spielberg probably has a lot to do with that.

It's funny. Harrison Ford's take on the wry, brilliant adventurer who would sacrifice his life not to lose his fedora is considered a classic performance.

It had a great female heroine. Marion is far from a damsel in distress: She can drink anyone under the table and hold her own in a fight.

It had boffo special effects, like the huge boulder that Indy runs from in the first scene, and the fire, ghosts, and melting heads in the final scene. Today, the effects seem kind of fake looking, but at the time they were spectacular.

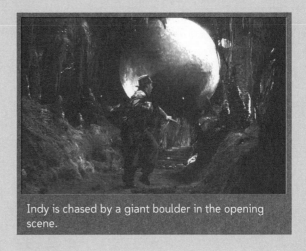

Indy is chased by a giant boulder in the opening scene.

Bonus Material

★ Tom Selleck was originally slated to play Indiana Jones, but his producers on the TV series *Magnum, P.I.* wouldn't release him from his contract; Harrison Ford was cast less than three weeks before filming started.

★ Indiana is the name of George Lucas' dog.

The opening scene: Indy and a guide are in a tomb replacing a gold idol they are stealing with an equally weighted bag of sand (so as to not set off an ancient booby trap). It works, and then it doesn't. What follows is several action-packed minutes during which Indy is betrayed by his partner, ducks poison darts, slides under a descending stone wall, and outruns a boulder the size of Saturn.

Indy's hat and whip: His fedora is a good luck charm he'll risk his life to keep, and he uses his whip to get out of all sorts of jams.

The sword-fighter scene: When Indy, who is in Cairo, is confronted by a scary sword-wielding man fully focused on chopping him to bits, he simply takes out a gun and shoots him. It's unexpected and very funny.

The chase scene: Intent on getting the Ark back from the Nazis, Indy climbs on, in, and under speeding trucks to secure the artifact.

The soundtrack: John Williams composed the historic soundtrack; same guy who did the music for *Hook*, the Harry Potter movies, *Star Wars*, and *Superman* (page 121).

QUOTABLES

"I hate snakes."

Indy says this after narrowly escaping death several times and then finding a snake, the only thing he's afraid of, in the cockpit of his getaway plane. (Snakes continue to plague him throughout the movie.)

MAD MAX 2: THE ROAD WARRIOR

DIRECTOR: GEORGE MILLER

SCREENWRITERS: TERRY HAYES, GEORGE MILLER, AND BRIAN HANNANT

WHAT IT'S ABOUT

It's some time in the future in a post-apocalyptic Australia, and a series of massive wars have turned the population into desperate, desert nomads in search of what is now the world's most precious resource: oil. In this sequel to the 1979 film *Mad Max*, gun-toting, leather pants-wearing Max Rockatansky (aka the Road Warrior) is a hardened former police officer who's lost all of his family and now roams the never-ending desert landscape in an old but tricked-out muscle car in search of gasoline. His travels lead him to a remote makeshift town, in which a small group of survivors owns hoards of this scarce resource. But their elaborate oil refinery is terrorized daily by a murderous, insane gang of bandits led by a masked tyrant named Lord Humungus.

The oil-owning clan members want to make it to the coast, where it is thought to be safe, but they need a way to take their vast supply of oil with them (something Humungus and his crew are not about to let happen). Max knows of a rig left in the desert and makes it clear the only way the townspeople are getting out of there alive is with his help. They pay him in oil to get the rig and bring it back, and then ask him to drive the rig with them to the coast—with Humungus and his evil crew at their tails.

Who's In It

Mel Gibson as Max Rockatansky

Bruce Spence as The Gyro Captain

Kjell Nilsson as Lord Humungus

Vernon Wells as Wez

Michael Preston as Pappagallo

Max Phipps as The Toadie

Emil Minty as The Feral Kid

More With Mel Gibson

Mad Max (1979)
Gallipoli (1981)
Lethal Weapon (1987)
Maverick (1994)
Braveheart (1995)

WHY ALL THE FUSS?

The Road Warrior is credited with inventing the post-apocalyptic junkyard aesthetic. The vehicles in the film are cobbled together from many different types of cars, motorcycles, and trucks, and this type of design element would later be seen in less successful movies including *Waterworld*, *The Postman*, and *Steel Dawn*, as well as in video games such as *Fallout*.

It's a fantastic action film. The energy rarely pauses, and the final chase scene, which is one of the most exhilarating movie chase scenes ever, takes up the whole last third of the film.

A young Mel Gibson is great as Max, the solitary, often unlikable hero who only speaks about a dozen lines in the movie. This movie pretty much made his career.

It was one of the first blockbuster films from Australia. This was a big deal at the time.

It was a huge commentary on war, fascism, and anarchy—as well as on humans' dependency on oil. The desolate world in the movie is filled with psychotic outlaws that seem to be a cross between pirates, Hells Angels, Nazis, and the like.

Bonus Material

★ The *South Park* episode "Proper Condom Use" includes a spoof on *The Road Warrior*. (The girls construct a compound similar to the one the townspeople do in the movie to keep the boys out after learning the boys can get them pregnant. The boys, of course, approach the compound on bikes à la Humungus and his gang.)

★ An entire culture sprang up out of the movie. *Road Warrior* conventions still take place, and people make replicas of Max's car, which was a tricked-out version of a 1973 Ford Falcon XB GT, for the events.

★ In 1985, a third movie in the series, *Mad Max Beyond Thunderdome*, was released. Singer Tina Turner played the role of Aunty Entity and sang the theme song "We Don't Need Another Hero (Thunderdome)."

★ Gibson went on to direct. His movies included *Braveheart* (which won the Academy Award for Best Picture) and the controversial *The Passion of the Christ*.

THE STUFF PEOPLE STILL TALK ABOUT

The meeting of Humungus: The mask-wearing, murderous leader and his band of thugs drive up to the settlers' compound on a fleet of cobbled-together vehicles and make it clear they're ready to fight.

The costumes: Humungus and his gang sport Technicolor-dyed hair, armor, helmets, masks, feathers, goggles, harnesses, and much more—and the result is a distinct and threatening look.

The feral kid: A young, mute little boy warrior lives with the settlers and uses a razor-sharp boomerang as a weapon, killing one of Humungus' followers and slicing off the fingers of another.

Mel's leather duds: Gibson's character travels the desert and does battle with his foes in a bad-ass leather getup.

Mad Max, decked out in his leather duds against the backdrop of a desert landscape.

QUOTABLES

"Two days ago I saw a vehicle that would haul that tanker. You want to get out of here? You talk to me."

Mad Max says this to the townspeople under siege by the lawless gang, knowing he is their only hope for escaping from Humungus with their oil.

"I am gravely disappointed. Again you have made me unleash my dogs of war."

Humungus says this to Mad Max, warning of bad things to come.

1982

BLADE RUNNER

DIRECTOR: RIDLEY SCOTT

SCREENWRITERS: HAMPTON FANCHER AND DAVID WEBB PEOPLES

WHAT IT'S ABOUT

It's Los Angeles in the year 2019 (which was seen as "futuristic" at the time of the movie). The world is a high-tech, industrial, neon-filled multicultural wasteland in which flying cars zip around and acid rain pours down almost nonstop. Humans have created androids that are faster, stronger versions of themselves called replicants, which were once used for slave labor and entertainment and now reside in "off-world" colonies because they have become a danger to Earth.

Unfortunately, four angry replicants—including warrior Rob and beauty Pris—rebel and make their way to Earth, intent on meeting with their creator, Dr. Eldon Tyrell, to find out if he can extend their preprogrammed four-year life span. They are inhumanly strong and primed for a killing spree. Rick Deckard, a retired blade runner (i.e., sanctioned assassin), is recruited to track down the group of renegade replicants. Rick starts battling them one by one in gory, action-packed scenes. He's coming out ahead, but he has another problem: He's falling in love with Rachael, Tyrell's beautiful assistant, who's also a replicant (though she doesn't know it). Rick's new crush is not ideal. For one, he's been asked to kill her. And second, he doesn't know how long she has to live. They do finally escape together, and we learn that Rachael was programmed differently from the others—and does not have the same four-year life span they do. That's a good thing, except that we don't really know for how long she was programmed to live.

Who's In It

Harrison Ford as Rick Deckard

Sean Young as Rachael

Rutger Hauer as Roy Batty

Edward James Olmos as Gaff

M. Emmet Walsh as Bryant

Daryl Hannah as Pris

More With Harrison Ford

American Graffiti (1973)
Star Wars (1977)
Raiders of the Lost Ark (1981, page 138)
Working Girl (1988)
Patriot Games (1992)
The Fugitive (1993)

WHY ALL THE FUSS?

Pris (center) checks out the weird, futuristic Los Angeles.

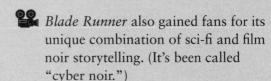 *Blade Runner* also gained fans for its unique combination of sci-fi and film noir storytelling. (It's been called "cyber noir.")

A special director's cut was released, which included added scenes and did away with the studio-imposed feel-good ending (in which Rick and Rachael ride off together into a beautiful landscape).

Blade Runner broke new ground with its depiction of a 21st century technological wasteland. Both the art direction and visual effects received Oscar nominations, and the movie's aesthetic was a precursor to futuristic sci-fi flicks like *The Matrix*, *Total Recall*, *Children of Men*, and the television series *Battlestar Galactica*.

 Blade Runner is based on Philip K. Dick's 1968 novel *Do Androids Dream of Electric Sheep?*

Bonus Material

★ Tensions were high on set. Reportedly, Harrison Ford did not get along with co-star Sean Young or director Ridley Scott.

★ At one point, Martin Scorsese considered buying the rights to the novel *Do Androids Dream of Electric Sheep?* so as to make a film out of it, but decided not to.

★ The landscape shots used at the end of the first theatrical version of the movie that was released are the same ones used in the opening sequence of *The Shining* (page 135).

The set design: An overbuilt, futuristic neon world is filled with clouds of fog and smoke, and special effects of flying cars and massive city landscapes.

The origami miniatures: A cop named Gaff has an odd habit of crafting tiny figures from paper and leaving them places. One ends up sending an important signal to Rick.

Rick's humanity: Many fans of the movie continue to debate whether Rick might have been a replicant himself.

QUOTABLES

"Sushi. That's what my ex-wife called me. Cold fish."

Rick Deckard says this as he sits down for a meal at the beginning of the movie. It very much has the feel of an old private eye film, but he's surrounded by a crazy futuristic street scene.

"I've seen things you people wouldn't believe. Attack ships on fire off the shoulder of Orion. I watched C-beams glitter in the darkness at Tan Hauser Gate. All those moments will be lost in time like tears in rain. Time to die."

The lead replicant, Roy, says this to Rick after they have engaged in a long fight and he is about to die. Even though he's not human, his point is very much so: He is saying that when he dies, all of his incredible experiences will die with him.

1983 SCARFACE

DIRECTOR: BRIAN DE PALMA

SCREENWRITER: OLIVER STONE

WHAT IT'S ABOUT

The first *Scarface* was originally made in 1932 by Howard Hawks. But the *Scarface* that went down in history was a 1983 remake starring the one and only Al Pacino. A pre-eminent gangster flick, it tells the story of Tony Montana, a Cuban refugee and criminal whose ambition is unyielding. After arriving in Florida, he quickly becomes involved in the drug trade and starts doing jobs for a kingpin named Frank Lopez. Frank sends Tony and this other guy, Omar, to Bolivia to negotiate a big deal with another drug heavy, Alejandro Sosa, but Alejandro ends up killing Omar and partnering with Tony—and Frank and Tony end their relationship.

Frank tries to take Tony out, but Tony solves the problem by killing Frank and proceeds to take over his business, marry Frank's girl-friend Elvira (whom he'd been aggressively pursuing), and become a zillionaire. Tony is living large—he owns a huge mansion and a tiger—but he's using his own product too much, and then gets bust-ed for money laundering. His old partner Alejandro offers to help him out, but Tony has to kill one of Alejandro's men in exchange, and he screws things up by not going through with it. Alejandro is pissed, and he dispatches an army of gun-toting guys to take Tony out. A paranoid, soulless, drug-addicted wreck, Tony defiantly strikes back in a final scene in which he takes on all of his assassins with a machine gun, killing most of them. However, he's finally shot and falls to his death, landing in the shallow pool of his mansion's foyer.

Who's In It

Al Pacino as
Tony Montana

Michelle Pfeiffer as
Elvira Hancock

Paul Shenar as
Alejandro Sosa

Mary Elizabeth Mastrantonio as
Gina Montana

Robert Loggia as
Frank Lopez

More With Al Pacino

The Godfather (1972, page 87)
Serpico (1973)
The Godfather: Part II (1974)
Dog Day Afternoon (1975)
Carlito's Way (1993)

More Written by Oliver Stone

Wall Street (1987)
Platoon (1986)
Natural Born Killers (1994)

WHY ALL THE FUSS?

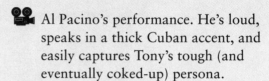

The violence is out of control. Tony's buddy is hacked to death by a chainsaw; Tony kills a man with a shot to his face on the street in broad daylight; yet another character is killed and hung out of a helicopter. There is also so much profanity that, if you eliminated it, the movie would last about 12 minutes.

Al Pacino's performance. He's loud, speaks in a thick Cuban accent, and easily captures Tony's tough (and eventually coked-up) persona.

It is a cocaine and violence-infused melodrama that also features music, fashion, and colorful settings (restaurants, clubs, drug dealer mansions, and the seedy streets) à la the tacky glamour of 1970s Miami.

QUOTABLES

"Say 'Hello' to my little friend."

Tony threatens the dozens of people who have been sent to kill him, as he unleashes a rain of bullets onto them.

"All I have in the world is my balls and my word, and I don't break them for no one."

Tony gives this testament of his own trustworthiness to a Bolivian drug lord when they are discussing a partnership.

THE STUFF PEOPLE STILL TALK ABOUT

Tony and Elvira out on the town.

★ A testament to the movie's enduring legacy, you can now own Tony Montana Halloween costumes, a *Scarface* "Say Hello to My Little Friend" ringtone, or watch the film's DVD documentary featuring hip-hop icons such as Snoop Dogg and P. Diddy talking about the *Scarface* philosophy. Or, you can buy the *Scarface* video game.

★ Elvira in *Scarface* was Michelle Pfeiffer's first dramatic role.

★ The comedian performing the routine at the nightclub before the assassination attempt on Tony is actor/comedian Richard Belzer, who played Detective John Munch in the series *Homicide: Life on the Street* and *Law & Order: Special Victims Unit.*

The final shoot-out scene: Now a big-time drug lord, Tony is at his compound coked out of his mind on his own product. He knows he's about to be ambushed by his rivals and is prepared to kill. He kicks open a door, machine gun in hand, and utters the movie's most famous line (see left). The rest is (very bloody) history.

The coke shot: Tony sits at his desk in his mansion with a ridiculous amount of cocaine in front of him. He's also got coke all over his face. It's an over-the-top moment of excess and shows he has hit rock bottom.

The chainsaw scene: A meeting with a drug dealer goes very wrong, and one of Tony's friends gets killed in a shower with a chainsaw.

THIS IS SPINAL TAP

DIRECTOR: ROB REINER

SCREENWRITERS: CHRISTOPHER GUEST, MICHAEL MCKEAN, ROB REINER, AND HARRY SHEARER

WHAT IT'S ABOUT

This Is Spinal Tap is a fictional documentary (a mockumentary) about Spinal Tap, a made-up, past-its-prime British heavy-metal band embarking on a tour promoting its latest release, "Smell the Glove." Filmmaker Marty DiBergi follows the band—which consists of social rejects Nigel, David, and Derek—on its journey, and captures behind-the-scenes candid interviews with the group members, as well as live performances that range from the ridiculous to the pathetic and uncomfortable (people don't show up, special effects constantly misfire). Along the way, the band members are reliably—and laughably—full of themselves and clueless about what big losers they are. They frequently say really stupid things (like "It's such a fine line between stupid and clever" and "Dozens of people spontaneously combust each year—it's just not really widely reported") and are not above padding the crotch area of their pants for the ladies.

Poor album sales and increasingly smaller crowds (as well as infighting among the band members) bring the tour to a disappointing end. Until, of course, Spinal Tap suddenly hits it big in Japan and is given yet another chance at rock god greatness.

Who's In It

Christopher Guest as Nigel Tufnel

Michael McKean as David St. Hubbins

Harry Shearer as Derek Smalls

Rob Reiner as Marty DiBergi

Tony Hendra as Ian Faith

More Directed by Rob Reiner

Stand by Me (1986)
The Princess Bride (1987)
When Harry Met Sally (1989)
Misery (1990)
A Few Good Men (1992)

WHY ALL THE FUSS?

 With pitch-perfect accuracy, it mocks the genre of rock documentaries, taking on movies such as the Beatles' *Let It Be*, the Band's *The Last Waltz*, and Bob Dylan's *Don't Look Back,* as well as the self-important and often ridiculous behavior of heavy-metal musicians and rock stars in general, as seen in many episodes of VH1's *Behind The Music*.

 The key to its success is that every scene, no matter how ridiculous, is played completely straight-faced. While other "mockumentaries" had been made before, this one was so convincing that some reviewers didn't realize it was a joke.

 Cast member Christopher Guest went on to direct and star in several other hilarious movies in a similar vein, including *Waiting for Guffman*, *Best in Show*, and *A Mighty Wind*.

Bonus Material

★ Much of the dialogue in the film was improvised by the actors.

★ The actors play their own instruments in the film; they even toured as Spinal Tap in the years following the movie.

QUOTABLES

"It isn't a college town."

The band's manager Ian Faith says this when explaining why a Boston tour stop has been canceled. (The joke: Boston is a *huge* college town.)

"These go to 11."

Band member Nigel says this when describing his oh-so-awesome and hard-core amps—which is ridiculous, because amps, of course, cannot "go to 11."

The Stonehenge scene: An 18-inch replica of Stonehenge is lowered onto the stage during a Spinal Tap performance. (It was supposed to be 18 *feet* high and very impressive; instead, it's puny and pathetic.)

The pod scene: The band members all emerge from cocoonlike capsules on stage for a song, but band member Derek Smalls gets trapped in his. It takes hammers and blowtorches to liberate him, but by the time he's freed, the song is over. Yet another special effect gone wrong.

The airport scene: Band member Derek Smalls gets busted at the airport for having a foil-wrapped pickle in his pants.

The many ridiculous songs: The band's tunes include "Big Bottoms" and "Sex Farm."

David, Derek, and Nigel singing (or screaming) their hearts out.

THE BREAKFAST CLUB
DIRECTOR: JOHN HUGHES
SCREENWRITER: JOHN HUGHES

WHAT IT'S ABOUT

Five teens representing some classic high school stereotypes—a jock (Andrew), a brain (Brian), a princess (Claire), a criminal (John), and a basket case (Allison)—are sentenced to Saturday detention for misbehaving at school (one taped the butt cheeks together of another student, one skipped class to go shopping, another brought a flare gun to school. One of them—the basket case—says she showed up because she had "nothing better to do.")

They start out hating each other, but as the day progresses (and they find a common enemy in the principal) they reveal more about themselves (troubled family lives, social pressures, feelings of loneliness), and the students realize they have more in common than they thought. Throughout the day, improbable romances begin to take shape, they escape the library and run around the school, and they blow off steam by smoking pot and dancing. By the end of the day the students have formed a deep bond but also wonder if they'll be friends when they return the next day to the "real" world of high school.

Who's In It

Molly Ringwald as
Claire Standish

Judd Nelson as
John Bender

Anthony Michael Hall as
Brian Johnson

Ally Sheedy as
Allison Reynolds

Emilio Estevez as
Andrew Clark

Paul Gleason as
Richard Vernon

More Directed by John Hughes

Sixteen Candles (1984)
Weird Science (1985)
Ferris Bueller's Day Off (1986)
Planes, Trains & Automobiles (1987)

More With Molly Ringwald

Sixteen Candles (1984)
Pretty in Pink (1986)
For Keeps? (1988)

WHY ALL THE FUSS?

 The Breakfast Club is one of the ultimate teen movies. Unlike most of the teen movies that had come before it, *The Breakfast Club* didn't find kids on a beach or getting killed while making out—it featured them talking to each other honestly about serious issues such as sex, drugs, suicide, and feelings of insecurity and alienation.

 The movie brought together members of what was later dubbed "The Brat Pack," a group of young and successful actors who were often in the same movies. (Other Brat Pack movies, many from *Breakfast Club* director John Hughes, include *Sixteen Candles*, *Weird Science*, *Pretty in Pink*, and *Ferris Bueller's Day Off*.)

Andrew and Brian, the jock and the brain, share a moment together.

★ Simple Minds wrote "Don't You (Forget About Me)" specifically for the movie.

★ Director John Hughes has a cameo at the end of the movie in the role of Brian's father.

★ A 1985 J. C. Penney back-to-school advertising campaign was based on *The Breakfast Club* and shows teens dancing as the movie's cast did.

THE STUFF PEOPLE STILL TALK ABOUT

The dancing scene: The kids rock out in the library, each in their own particular style, to the song "We Are Not Alone."

The dandruff moment: Ally Sheedy as Allison uses her own dandruff to create snow for a drawing of a winter scene.

The lipstick scene: Claire shows a trick she learned at camp—putting on her lipstick with no hands (she puts it in her cleavage.)

"Don't You (Forget About Me)": This Simple Minds song comes on at the end of the film. It became synonymous with the movie, and with the idea of the fleeting years of high school.

QUOTABLES

"Does Barry Manilow know that you raid his wardrobe?"
John Bender says this to Principal Vernon to mock him.

Brian: "You wear tights?"
Andrew: "No I don't wear tights. I wear the required uniform."
Brian: "Tights."
Brian says this to Andrew about his wrestling outfit.

Allison: "Why are you being so nice to me?"
Claire: "Because you're letting me."
Claire and Allison have a bonding moment when Claire gives Allison a makeover.

"Oh, it's a fat girl's name."
John is talking about Claire's name in his very rough-around-the-edges way of flirting with her.

DO THE RIGHT THING

DIRECTOR: SPIKE LEE

SCREENWRITER: SPIKE LEE

WHAT IT'S ABOUT

It's the hottest day of the year in the poor black Brooklyn neighborhood of Bed-Stuy. A black young man named Mookie (played by director Spike Lee) works as a delivery boy at a pizzeria owned by a white Italian guy named Sal and is friendly with pretty much everyone in the neighborhood regardless of race. Characters in the neighborhood include Da Mayor, an older black guy who enjoys a midday beer; Mother Sister, an older black woman who sits in her window all day observing the activity below; Radio Raheem, a big dude who walks around with a giant boom box blasting Public Enemy; three wise-cracking guys who sit on the corner all day busting on each other; and the local Korean grocers.

Sal, who's been serving the neighborhood for 25 years, decorates his pizza place with photos of his heroes (guys like Frank Sinatra). The thing is, they're all white, and that rubs some of his customers—most of whom are black—the wrong way. Over the course of a single day, tensions steadily increase, and Sal is the first to snap by taking a baseball bat to a rap-blaring boom box, intentionally brought in to the shop by two black guys. A huge fight breaks out, the police show up, and one of the black guys ends up dead. Out of frustration and rage, Mookie throws a garbage can through the pizzeria window, and an angry mob destroys the pizzeria. But the greatest damage is done to the sense of community in the neighborhood, and to close relationships such as Sal and Mookie's.

Who's In It

Spike Lee as
Mookie

Danny Aiello as
Sal

Bill Nunn as
Radio Raheem

Ossie Davis as
Da Mayor

Ruby Dee as
Mother Sister

Rosie Perez as
Tina

John Turturro as
Pino

Samuel L. Jackson as
Mister Señor Love Daddy

More Directed by Spike Lee

She's Gotta Have It (1986)
Jungle Fever (1991)
Malcolm X (1992)
Crooklyn (1994)
Summer of Sam (1999)
Bamboozled (2000)
Inside Man (2006)

WHY ALL THE FUSS?

Do the Right Thing is one of the most thought-provoking movies about race in America and really got people talking about the heart of the matter. It was also controversial because some people thought it encouraged violence in the face of racism.

Spike Lee's characters are complex and so are the situations they find themselves in. No one is presented as "good" or "bad" and, despite the title, the movie never states what "the right thing" to do is. It's upsetting (a community and long-time friendships are destroyed) and violent (a riot happens, someone is killed) and sad (because there doesn't seem to be a solution to the situation).

It established Lee as a filmmaker who made smart, provocative movies about race relations in America.

The movie also captured the feeling of summer in a New York City neighborhood, showing people hanging out on their stoops, kids playing in the stream of an open fire hydrant, and ice cream trucks coming down the block.

Bonus Material

★ Although nominated for two Oscars (Danny Aiello for Best Supporting Actor and Spike Lee for Best Screenplay), the movie was overlooked for Best Picture. Kim Basinger presented the Best Picture award at the Oscars and paused to comment that its absence in the category was a glaring omission. She was hissed at from the balcony.

★ Radio Raheem's "Love" and "Hate" rings are a call-out to the tattoos on Robert Mitchum's hands in *The Night of the Hunter*.

★ Barack and Michelle Obama saw *Do the Right Thing* on their first date.

THE STUFF PEOPLE STILL TALK ABOUT

Mookie throwing a trash can through Sal's pizzeria window: This act leads to mass rioting.

The opening credits: Rosie Perez delivers a high-energy performance boxing and dancing to the Public Enemy track "Fight the Power."

The racist rants: A section of the movie includes several different characters of different races looking straight at the camera and listing off countless slurs and racial stereotypes.

The bold, bright colors: As dark as the content seemed, the movie was also colorful, lively, and human.

Mookie on his way to deliver a pizza in Bed-Stuy.

QUOTABLES

"Let me tell you the story of 'Right Hand, Left Hand.' It's a tale of good and evil. Hate: It was with this hand that Cane iced his brother. Love: These five fingers, they go straight to the soul of man. The right hand: the hand of love."

Radio Raheem talks poetically about the fight between love and hate in the world.
(He has gold knuckle rings on his hands spelling out "love" and "hate.")

GOODFELLAS
DIRECTOR: MARTIN SCORSESE
SCREENWRITERS: NICHOLAS PILEGGI AND MARTIN SCORSESE

WHAT IT'S ABOUT

Henry Hill is a young kid in New York who does small jobs for the neighborhood gangsters. He loves it and drops out of school to do it full time. As an adult, he's taken into the fold and helps pull off bigger jobs. He loves the life of a "big shot" and strutting around at fancy clubs where he's treated like a king with his new girlfriend, Karen, who soon becomes his wife.

As he gets more and more involved with his gangster buddies, his life gets more dangerous and he also cheats on Karen (she finds out). When a job in Miami gets him busted, he's sent to jail for several years, from where he starts dealing—and taking—drugs. When he gets out, he ramps up his drug business, but things start going wrong and he has trouble keeping it all together. He turns into a drug-addled mess, and one afternoon as he's running several business-related errands (and trying to cook a big family dinner), he suspects he's being followed by the Feds. He's right. Busted, completely broke, and with his family in danger, he must decide if he'll rat out his friends and become a member of the Witness Protection Program or be a wiseguy to the end. He betrays his friends by talking to the FBI, many of his old buddies go to jail, and he moves to the middle of nowhere where he lives, as he sees it, the boring life of a nobody.

Who's In It

Ray Liotta
as Henry Hill

Robert De Niro as
James "Jimmy" Conway

Joe Pesci as
Tommy DeVito

Lorraine Bracco as
Karen Hill

Paul Sorvino as
Paul Cicero

Frank Sivero as
Frankie Carbone

Frank Vincent as
Billy Batts

More Directed by Martin Scorsese

Taxi Driver (1976, page 103)
Raging Bull (1980)
The King of Comedy (1982)
After Hours (1985)
Casino (1995)
The Departed (2006)

Goodfellas is based on screenwriter Nicholas Pileggi's 1985 novel *Wise Guy.*

WHY ALL THE FUSS?

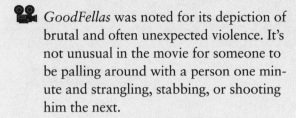 *GoodFellas* was noted for its depiction of brutal and often unexpected violence. It's not unusual in the movie for someone to be palling around with a person one minute and strangling, stabbing, or shooting him the next.

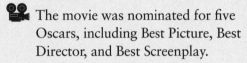 The movie was nominated for five Oscars, including Best Picture, Best Director, and Best Screenplay.

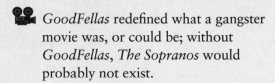 *GoodFellas* redefined what a gangster movie was, or could be; without *GoodFellas*, *The Sopranos* would probably not exist.

The movie thoroughly paints a picture of a way of life, from the rapid-fire dialogue and speech patterns of its characters, to the tacky furnishings and clothing of the 1950s and 60s, to the inner workings of a tight-knit criminal operation.

Bonus Material

★ The final shot of the movie features Henry Hill coming out his front door in a bathrobe to pick up the paper; this is directly referenced in the opening credits to the series *The Sopranos*, with Tony Soprano doing the same thing.

★ The "I amuse you?" scene was based on a story that actually happened to Joe Pesci; the dialogue was the result of an improvisation, which then became real lines in the script.

THE STUFF PEOPLE STILL TALK ABOUT

The graphically violent scenes: A guy who aggressively hits on Karen is standing in his driveway one minute and getting his face bashed in with a pistol the next; Billy Batts is having drinks at a bar and joking around, and then suddenly being kicked and pummeled to death on the floor. Then, there's the guy in the trunk of the car who's still alive and shouldn't be…you get the idea.

The body montage: The bodies of various victims of mob hits are found in locations such as a garbage truck and a meat locker.

Tommy goes crazy in the bar one night and shoots Spider, the young bartender.

The "I amuse you?" scene: Big gangster Tommy (Joe Pesci) is telling a story, and Henry tells him that he's funny. Tommy seems to take it the wrong way (saying, "I amuse you?"), and the air gets very tense as we wonder whether Tommy is going to pull out a gun and shoot Henry for simply saying that he's funny. Fortunately for Henry, Tommy's just kidding.

The Spider scenes: A young guy named Spider is serving the gangsters drinks at a poker game, and crazy Tommy shoots him in the foot for not bringing him his drink fast enough. The next poker night, the young guy has a cast on his foot. Tommy teases him, he curses at Tommy, and Tommy simply shoots him dead.

THE STUFF PEOPLE STILL TALK ABOUT

The entrance to the club: As Henry and Karen enter a nightclub for a date, they are followed in an extremely long, unbroken tracking shot that starts outside the club, goes through a side entrance, down a basement hallway, and to a table right in front of the stage—that's being set up for them just as they are ready to sit down.

Joe Pesci's performance: There really isn't a bad performance in this movie, but Pesci as the completely insane, unpredictable, and despicable Tommy is especially memorable. He won the Best Supporting Actor Oscar.

★ A young Michael Imperioli (Christopher in *The Sopranos*) plays the kid shot in the foot by Tommy. Lorraine Bracco (Dr. Jennifer Melfi from *The Sopranos*) plays Karen, Henry's wife.

★ Director Martin Scorsese's mother plays Tommy DeVito's mother in the film.

QUOTABLES

"I amuse you? I make you laugh, I'm here to fuckin' amuse you?"

Tommy's famous line to Henry (see page 161).

"Go home and get your fucking shine box."

Gangster Billy Batts taunts rival gangster Tommy DeVito, by referring to when Tommy was a shoe shine boy. The comment leads to Batts' murder.

WHAT IT'S ABOUT

FBI trainee Clarice Starling is instructed to meet with imprisoned serial killer Dr. Hannibal "The Cannibal" Lecter in an effort to track down Buffalo Bill, who is suspected of kidnapping the daughter of an important politician. Hannibal is terrifyingly creepy and finds strange ways to play with Clarice's head, but in the interest of the case, she continues to visit him. Lecter recognizes Clarice's talent and intelligence and forms a strange attachment to her. Little by little, he gives her more insight and riddles that help shed light on the investigation.

Through her exchanges with Lecter, Clarice eventually closes in on Bill and his victim. She finds herself without backup at his house, discovers the hostage, and is suddenly plunged into total darkness. Meanwhile, Bill puts on night-vision glasses, watches her stumble around his lair, and prepares to kill her. From here on out, a horrific showdown takes place. In the end, Clarice survives and is inducted into the FBI. But she does receive one final phone call from Lecter, who escaped with a characteristically gruesome and murderous scheme and is now in a tropical (presumably very far away) place. Before he hangs up he tells her "I'm having an old friend for dinner." Which with him, can only mean one thing…

The Silence of the Lambs is based on Thomas Harris' 1988 novel of the same name.

Who's In It

Jodie Foster as
Clarice Starling

Anthony Hopkins as
Dr. Hannibal Lecter

Scott Glenn as
Jack Crawford

Anthony Heald as
Dr. Frederick Chilton

Ted Levine as
Jame "Buffalo Bill" Gumb

Brooke Smith as
Catherine Martin

More Directed by Jonathan Demme

Something Wild (1986)
Married to the Mob (1988)
Philadelphia (1993)
Rachel Getting Married (2008)

More With Anthony Hopkins

Howards End (1992)
The Remains of the Day (1993)
Nixon (1995)
Meet Joe Black (1998)

WHY ALL THE FUSS?

The Silence of the Lambs was the first horror movie to win the Academy Award for Best Picture. (It also essentially swept the awards, taking home additional statues for Best Director, Best Screenplay, Best Actor, and Best Actress). Only two other movies in the history of the awards had been awarded all five Oscars in the major categories. (*It Happened One Night* in 1934, and *One Flew Over the Cuckoo's Nest* in 1975).

This is one terrifying, suspenseful movie—you can't not be scared by it. (Or, at the very least, really creeped out.) Hopkins as Lecter ranks up there as one of the scariest villains in cinema, and the climactic scene—featuring an androgynous, vain, and deranged sociopath outfitted with night-vision goggles—is not something you want to watch alone.

Foster is pretty unforgettable as the vulnerable and ambitious Clarice who forms a bond with a sociopath.

QUOTABLES

"A census taker once tried to test me. I ate his liver with some fava beans and a nice chianti."
Hannibal Lecter says this to Clarice, after she's pressed him for information, indicating he's not one to be messed with.

"It rubs the lotion on its skin. It does this whenever it is told."
Buffalo Bill says this to his captive Catherine, instructing her—"it"—to moisturize herself.

THE STUFF PEOPLE STILL TALK ABOUT

Hannibal "The Cannibal" Lecter wearing his face guard, which is supposed to stop him from eating people.

Hannibal Lecter's most terrifying moments: Locked within a high-security prison, he uses creepy psychological tactics to get inside Clarice's head and talks with pleasure about eating someone's liver. He also kills a man, skins his face off, and wears it in a gruesome, clever, and successful escape plot.

The crazy Buffalo Bill scene: A murderous, deranged transsexual named Buffalo Bill prepares to kill his latest captive, dressing up, applying makeup, and posing in the mirror with the song "Goodbye Horses" playing in the background.

Bonus Material

★ Hannibal Lecter was such a huge character when the movie came out that Billy Crystal, 1992's Academy Awards host, opened the show that year strapped to a gurney and wearing a muzzle—a gag inspired by Lecter and the movie.

★ Michelle Pfeiffer turned down the role of Clarice Starling.

★ The movie made Demme a Hollywood player. Prior to *Silence*, he was known for smaller indie movies such as the Talking Heads' concert film *Stop Making Sense* and Spalding Gray's *Swimming to Cambodia*.

Mimi O'Connor is a freelance writer and editor based in Brooklyn, New York. Under the name Lois Beckwith, she is the author of *The Dictionary of Corporate Bullshit* and Zest Books' *The Dictionary of High School B.S.* She also adapted *The Dictionary of Corporate Bullshit* for the 2008 and 2009 Page-A-Day Calendars.

ACKNOWLEDGMENTS FROM THE AUTHOR

Many thanks go out to the Zest team, especially Karen Macklin and Hallie Warshaw for all their support, keen questions, and patience. (And for allowing a few movies—that shall not be named here—to remain in the book.)

Thanks also to the Movie Book Think Tank, who generously riffed on all these great films: Elle "Don't Call Me Shirley" Chan, Lisa "Beavis" Deboer, Kelly Anne "Fanny Ekdahl" Keenan, Gretchen "Ursa" Kunz, Ramlah "Springfield" Lauritsen, Kevin "Jerry Blake" Maher, Jerome J. "Norma Desmond" O'Neill, Sarah "Karen Hill" Welt, Ken "Eraserhead" Wilson, Miss Eva Fwae "Tess McGill" Jung Yun, and Kate "Elwood Blues" Yun.

Great gratitude to Team 14 Bergen: Jonah "Rupert Pupkin" Kaplan and Cuomo (aka "Spock").